YOU GET THE PICTURE

By

Jeanne "Bean" Murdock

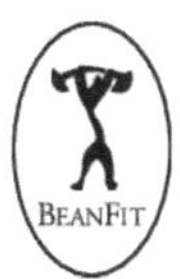

BEANFIT Publishing
Sedona, AZ
USA

Library of Congress Control Number: 2023906693
ISBN: 9798986094823

Photos taken by Jeanne "Bean" Murdock unless otherwise noted.

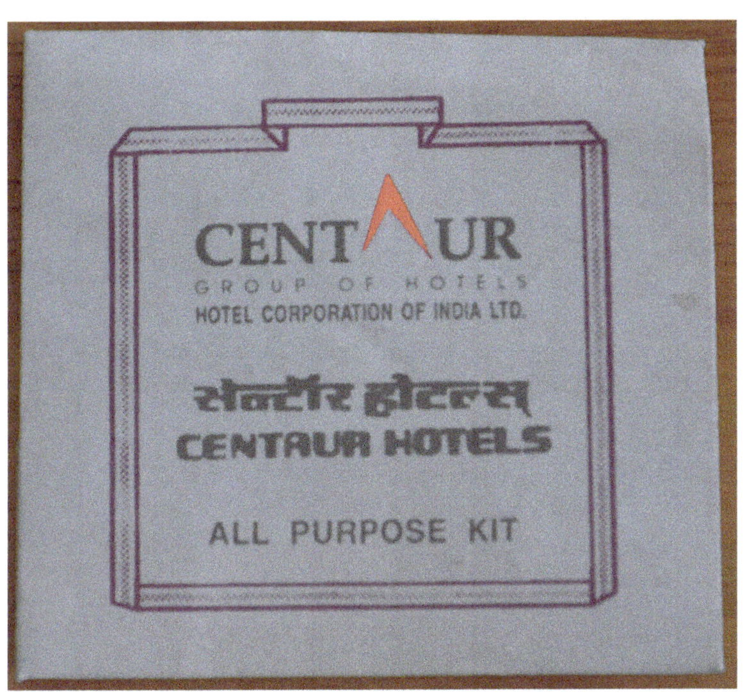

Condom enclosed.

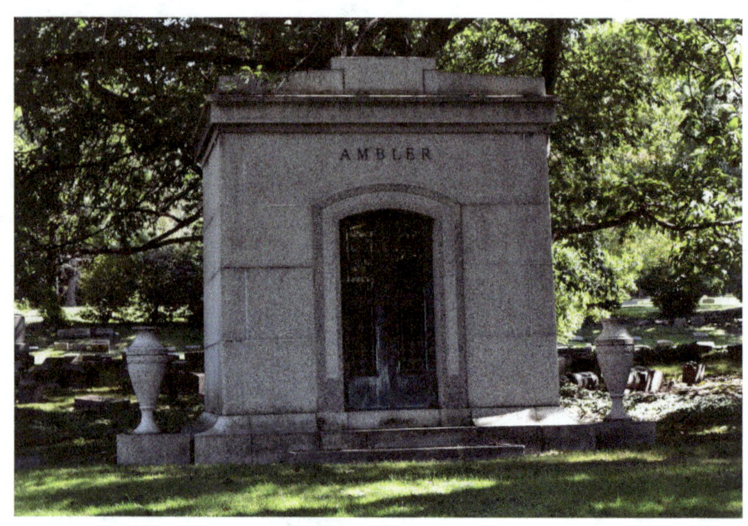

Not anymore.

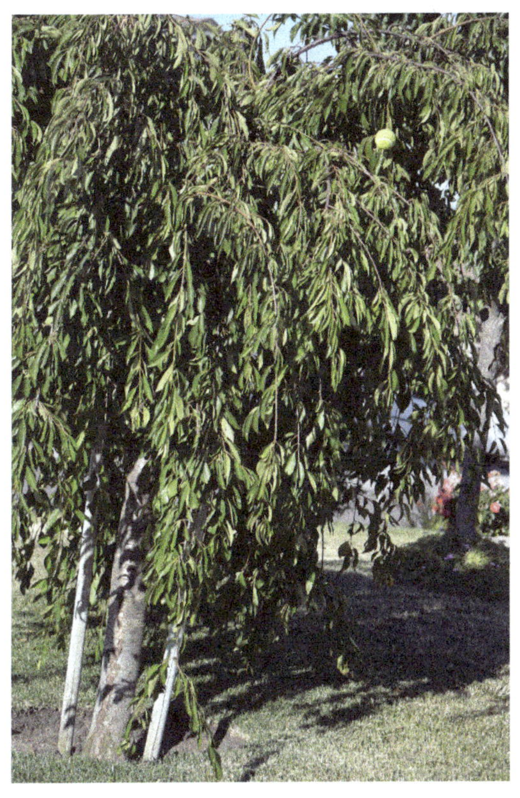

Dog's dream: Tennis balls grow on trees.

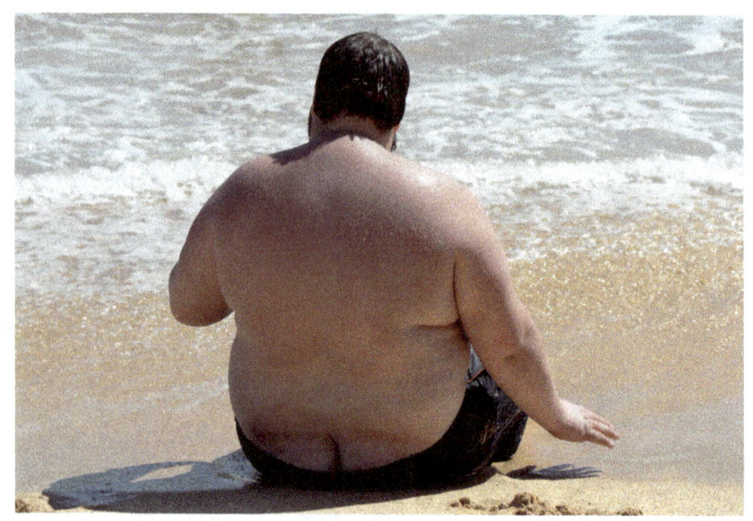

Beached bum.

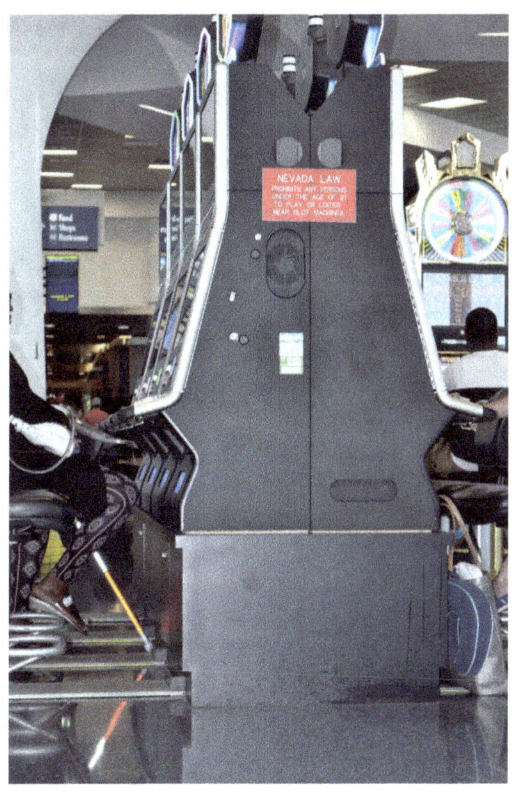

Blind luck.

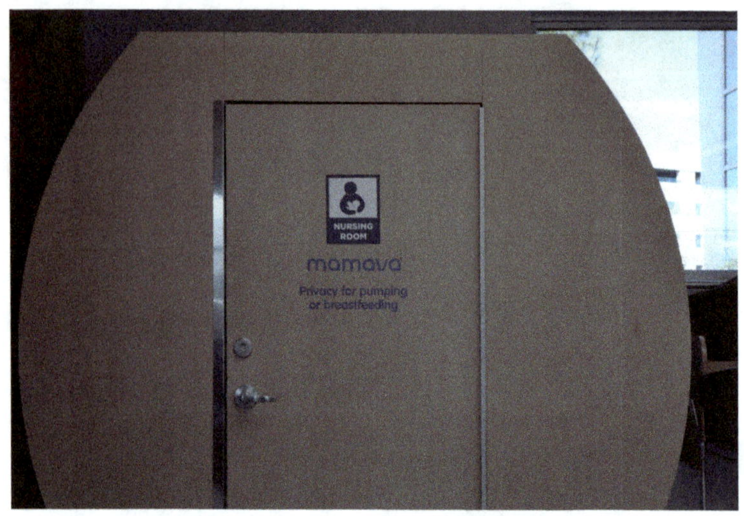

Breastfeeding mothers should be out of sight and locked in a dungeon.

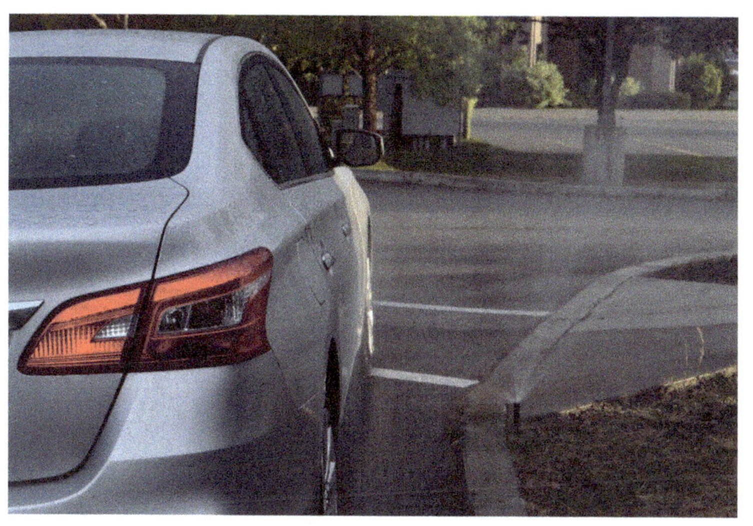

Redneck car wash.

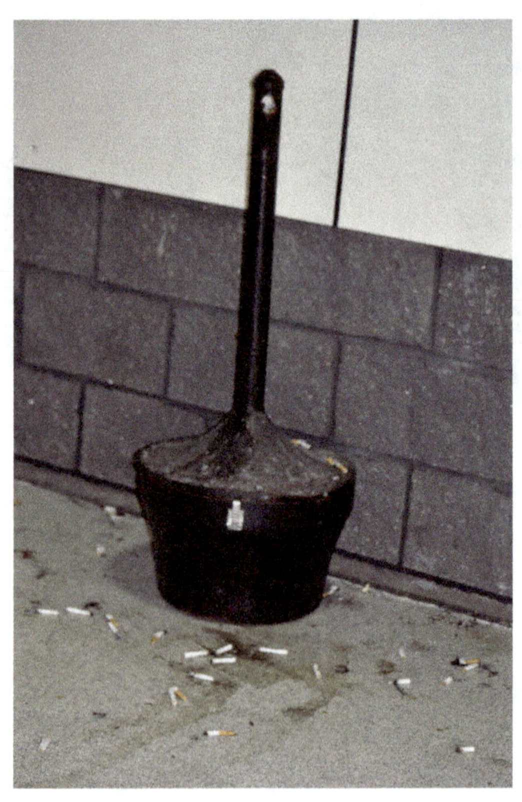

Epitome of lazy.

;. ✓ **Will Call C.O.D.** (All instances when credit has not been approved by DLE).
All C.O.D. Consumers are required to prepay for the propane delivery, including any outstanding
alance(s) on your account, before any deliveries are made. It is the Consumer's responsibility to
...the Company when the percentage gauge on the top of your propane

If you want people to pre-pay, then don't call it C. O. D. Call it C. B. D.—collect before delivery.

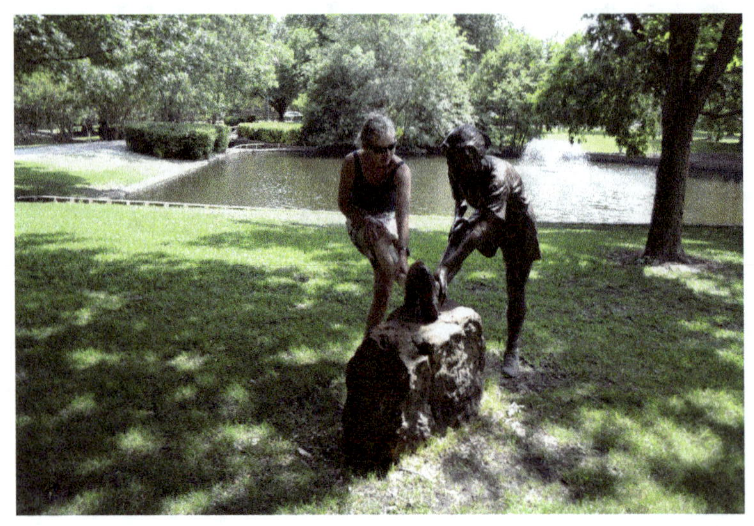

I still teach everywhere I go—even to statues.
Photo credit: Cooper Institute.

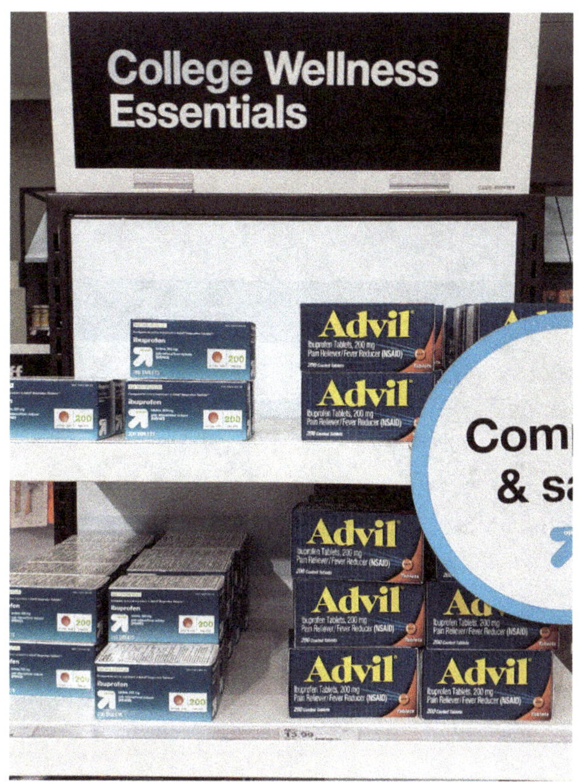

Addicted learning.

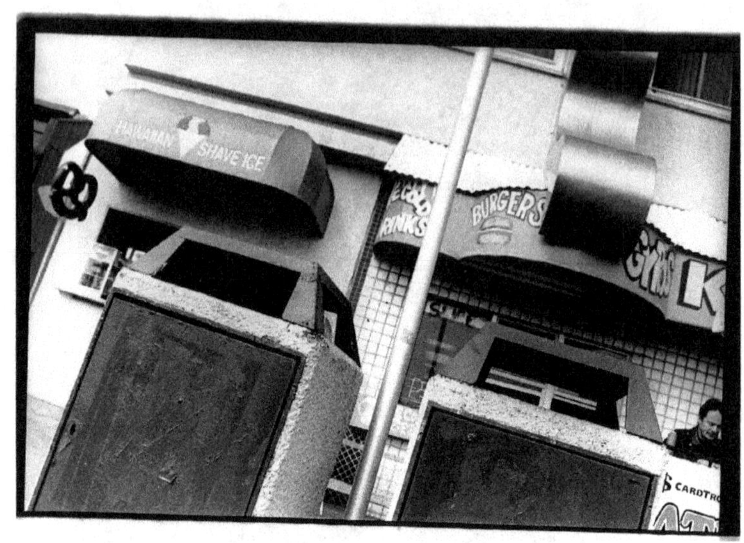

Dump bad habits.

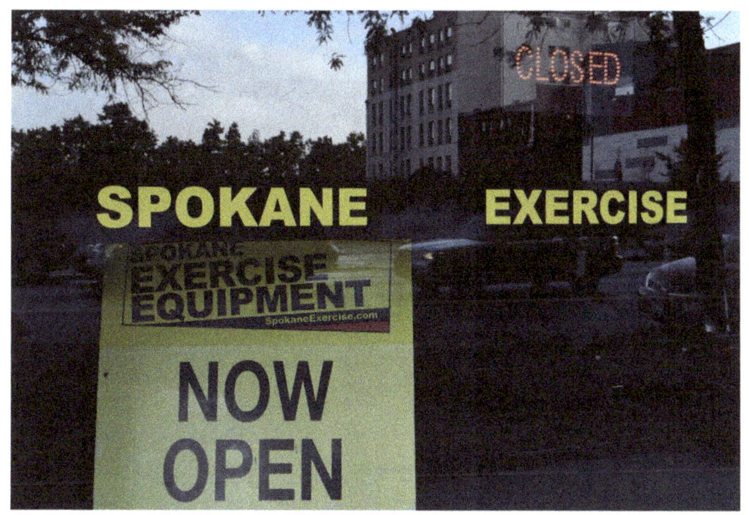

An open and closed case.

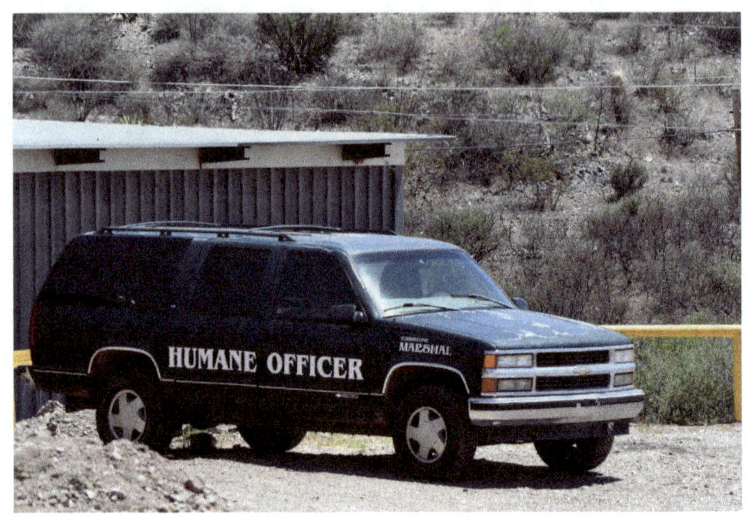

I would hope so.

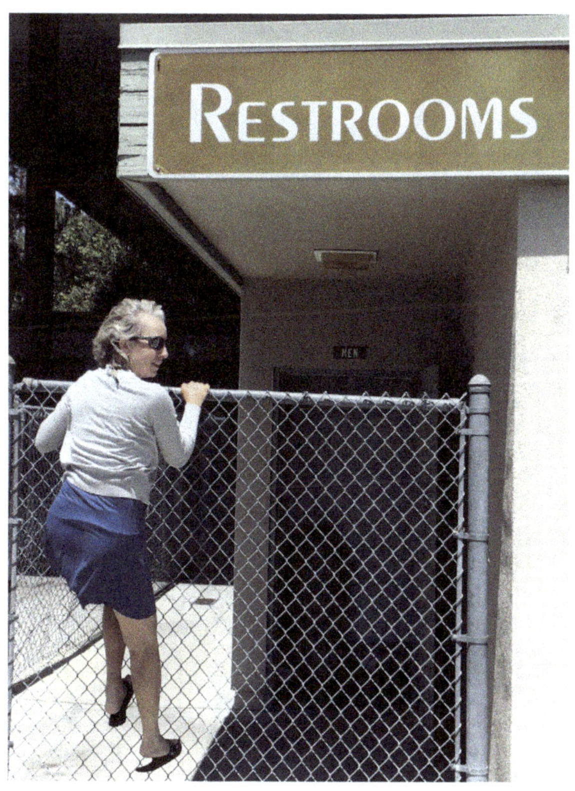

I'm on the fence about transgender restrooms.
Photo credit: C. C.

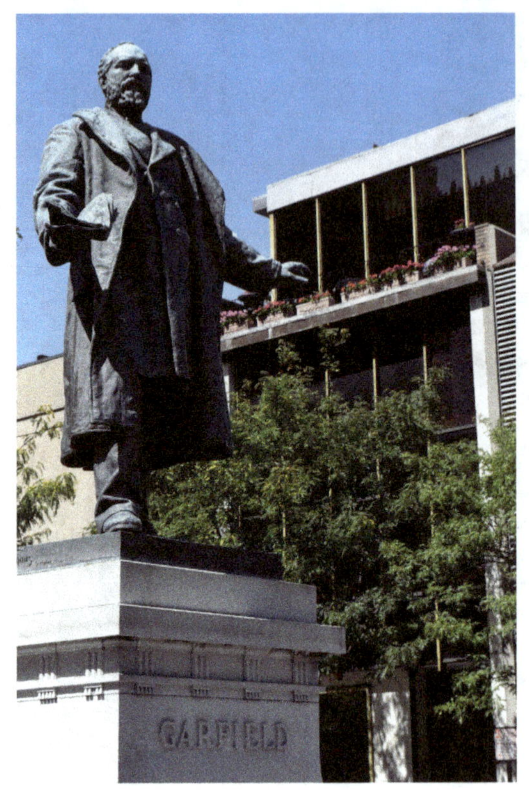

Even President Garfield picked flowers.

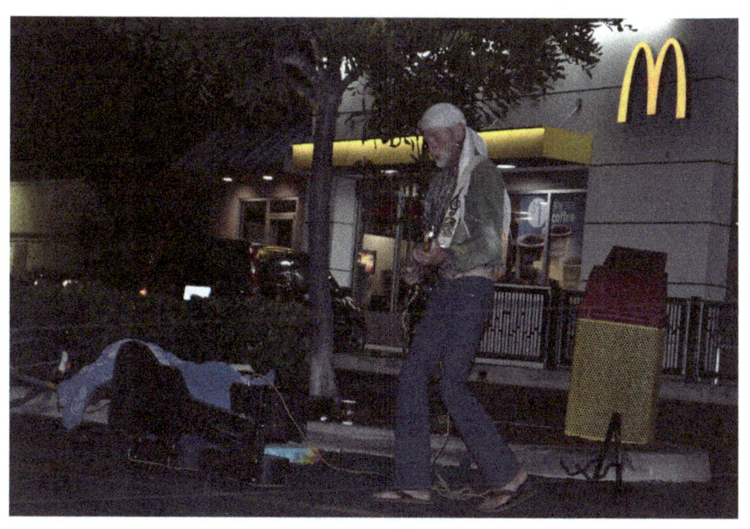

Rockin' off a meal.

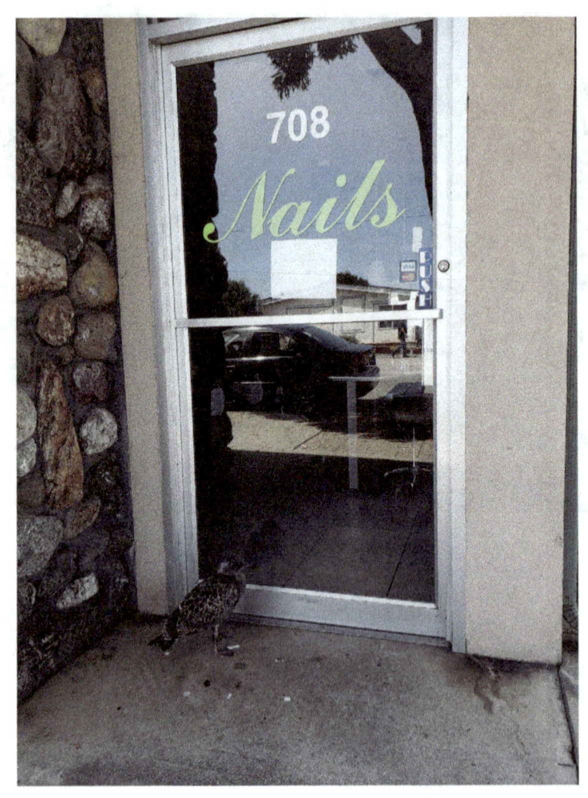

Even birds need a little pampering.

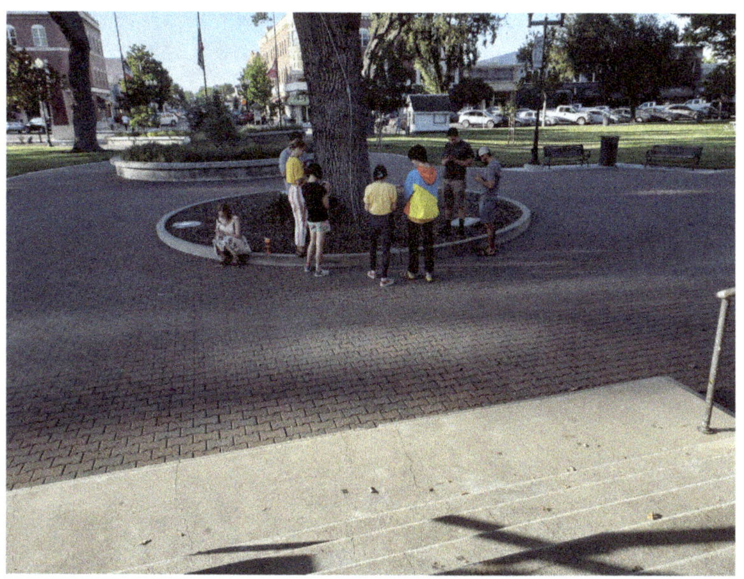

Teens . . . before intervention.

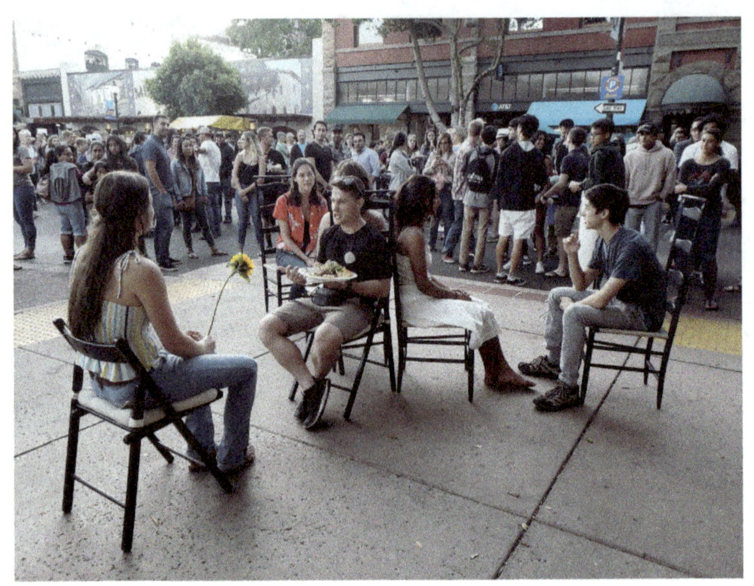

Teens . . . after intervention.

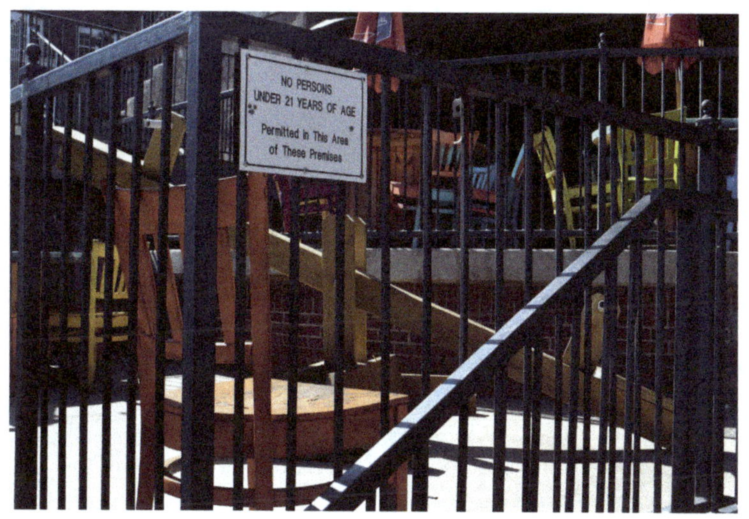

But there’s a teeter totter!

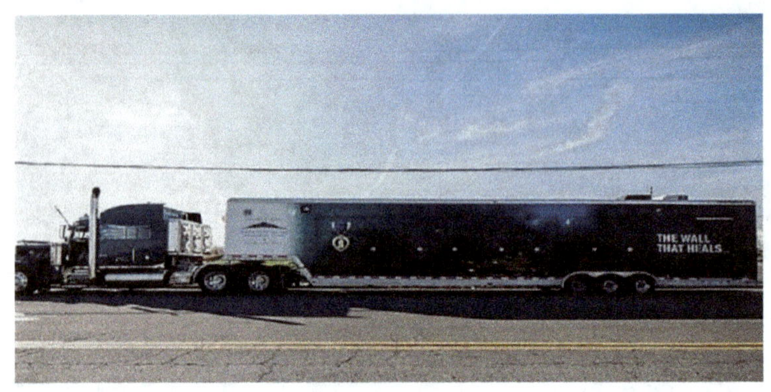

"The wall that heals":
nickname for the US/Mexican border wall.

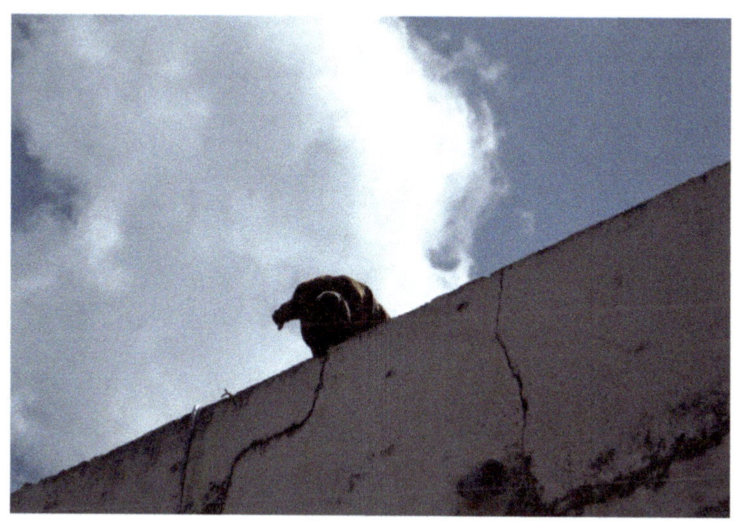

Watch dog.

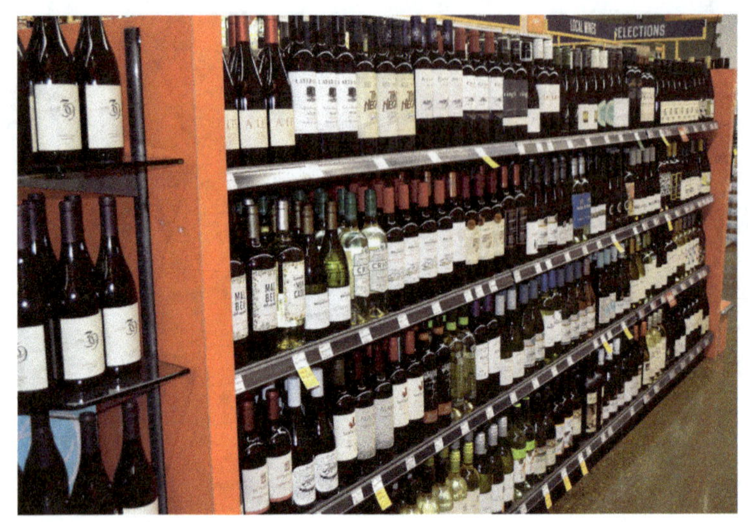

Alcohol in a health food store.
Aisle 8 has cocaine.
Marijuana is on 420.

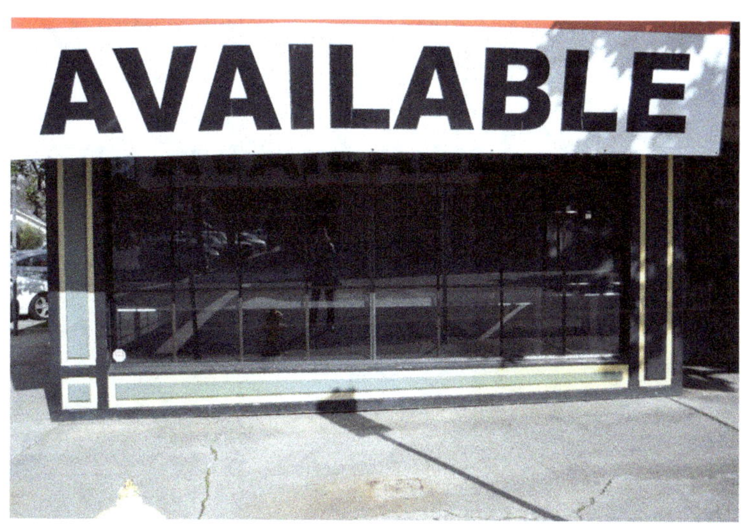

This sign hangs outside my home.

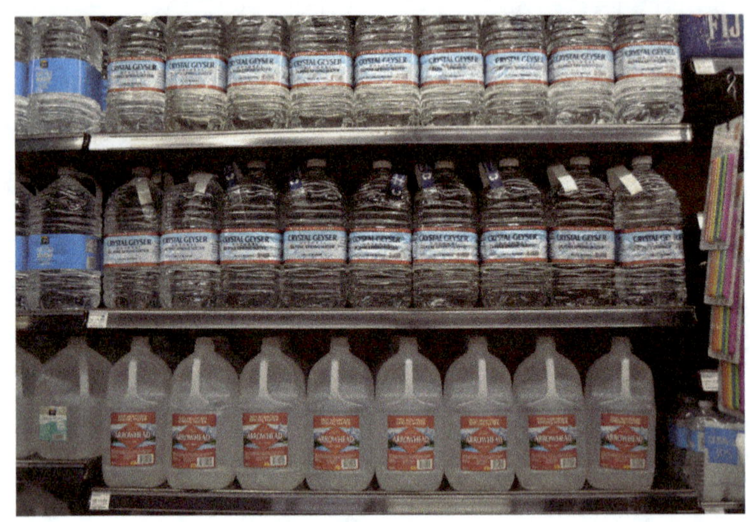

Energy drinks.

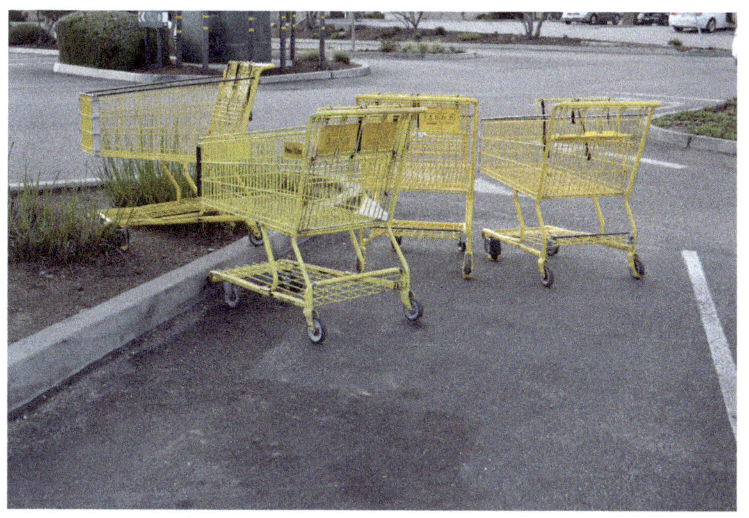

Laziness causes cart congestion and another congestion: congestive heart failure.

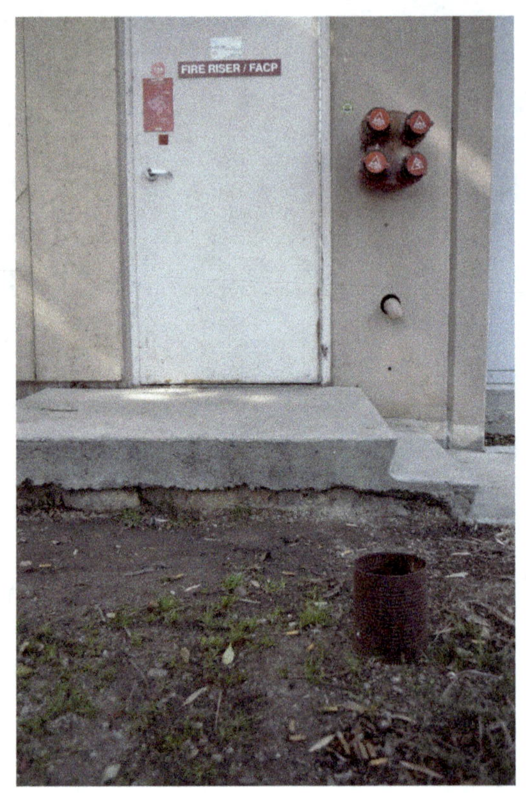

Health food store smoking section.

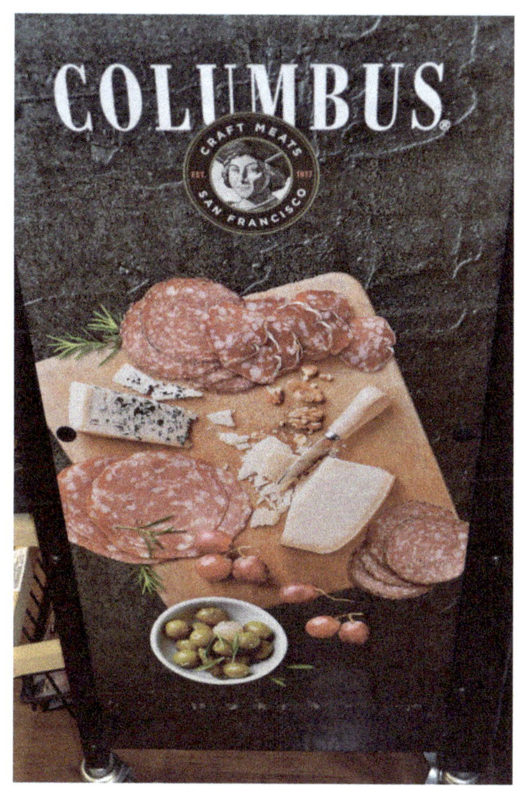

Now Columbus takes credit for discovering San Francisco . . . and salami.

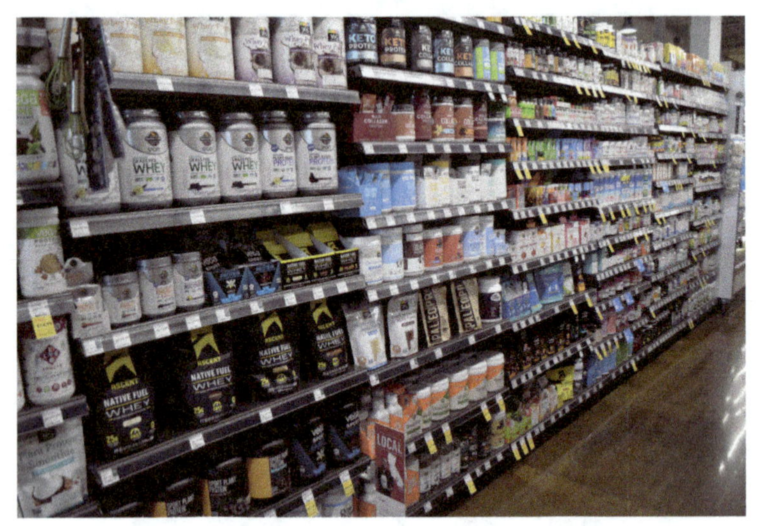

Darwin's unnatural selection.

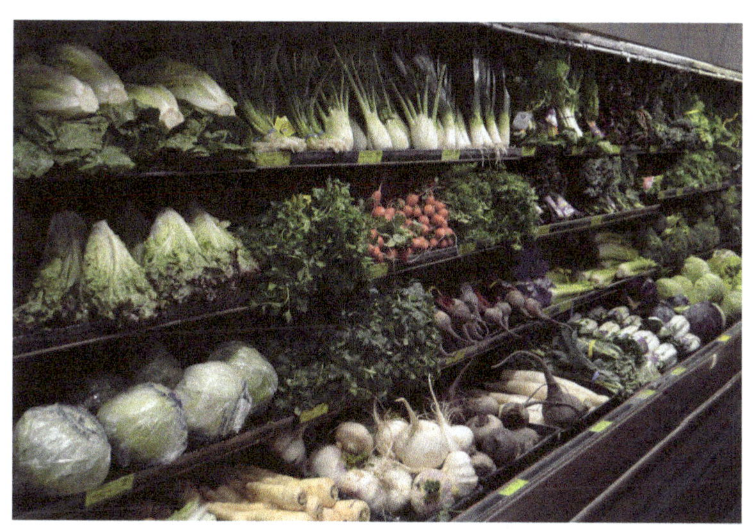

Darwin's natural selection.

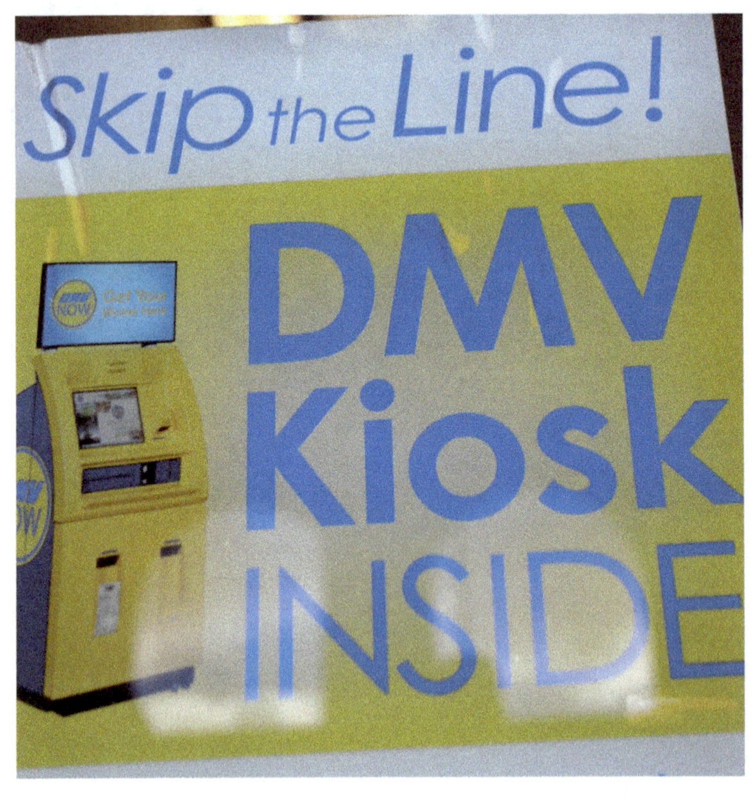

There wasn't a line, but I still waited hours for my number to be called and then I left.

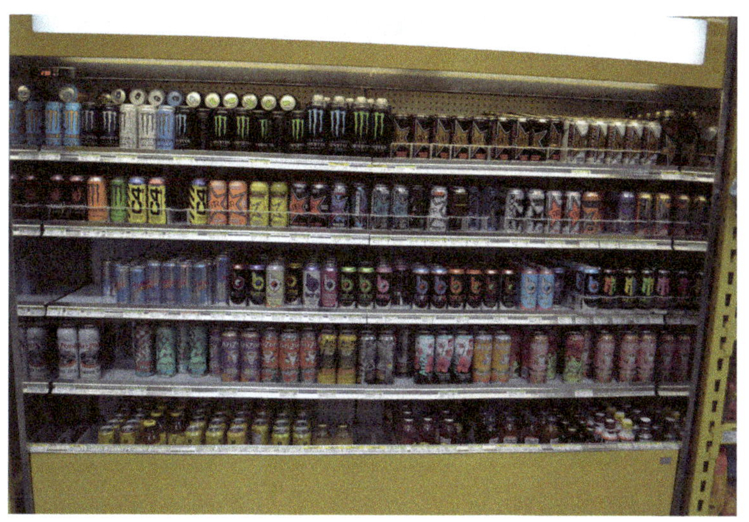

Energy-depleting drinks.

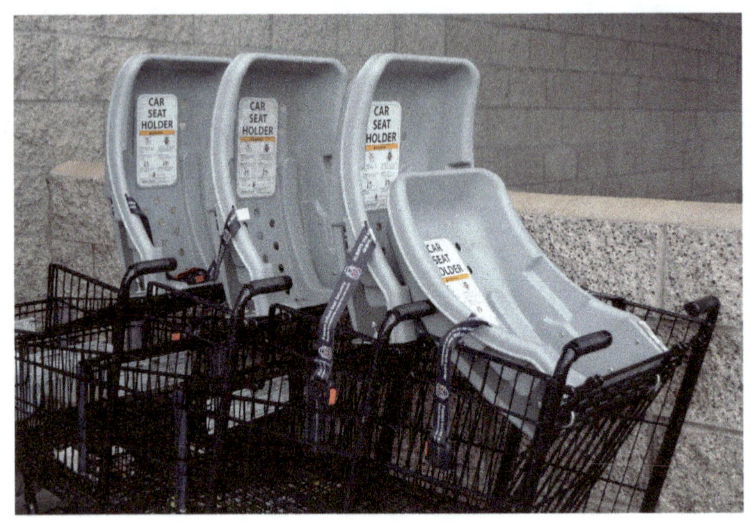

Ejection seats.

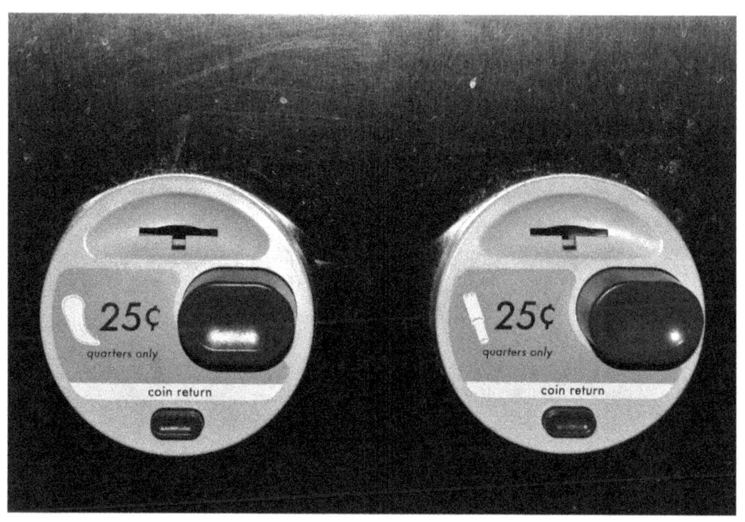

Child's perspective:
candy machine in the women's restroom.

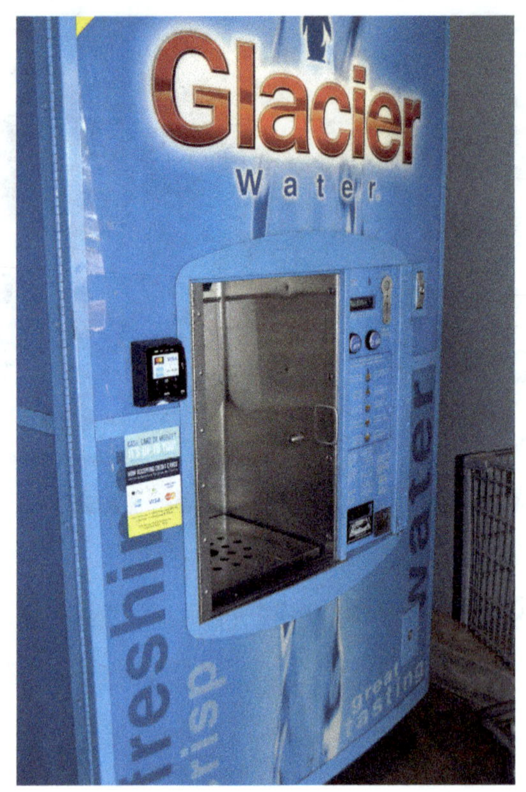

America is a third-world country.
Homes don't have potable water.

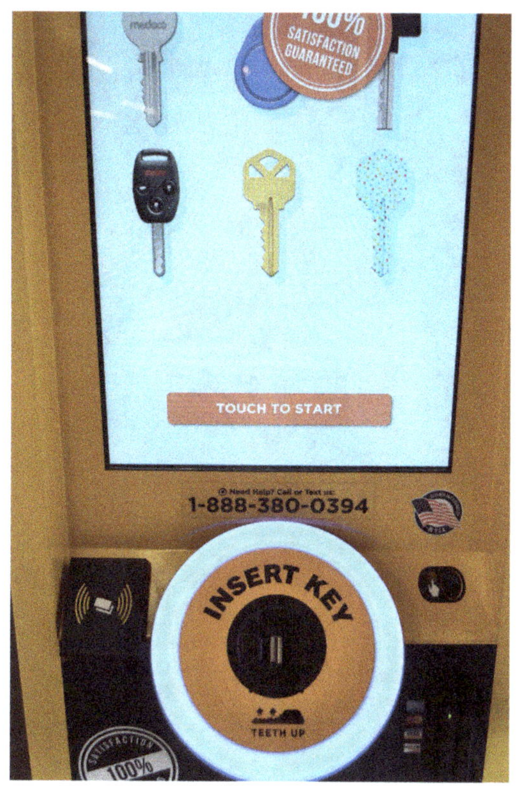

After I inserted my house key, I had to enter my address.

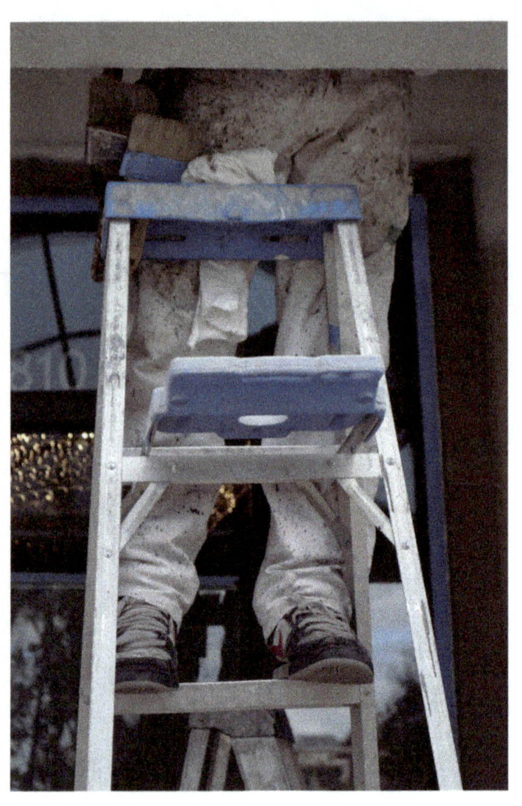

Painter’s pants.

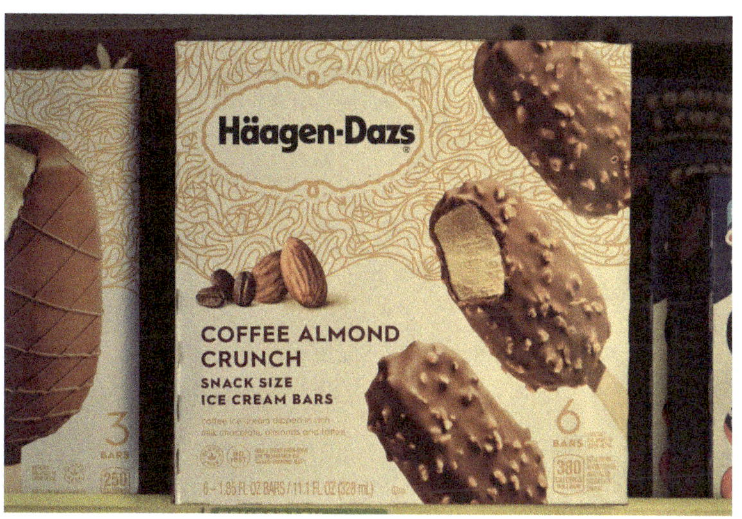

Snack size, as opposed to meal size.

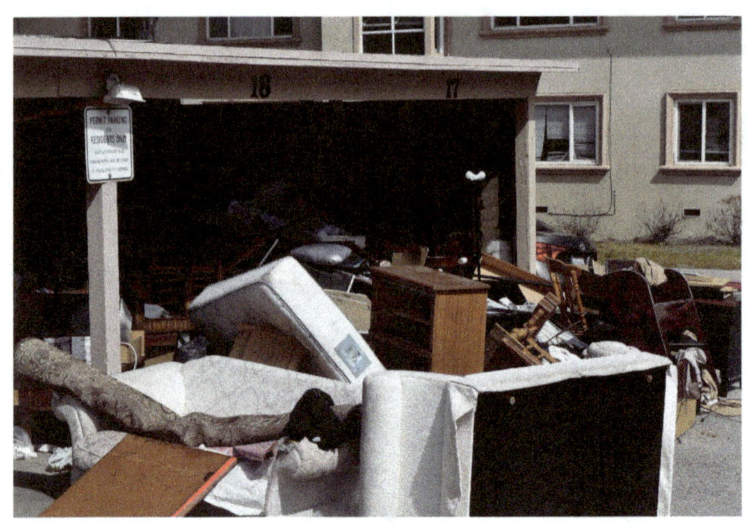

Dumping is PERMITable.

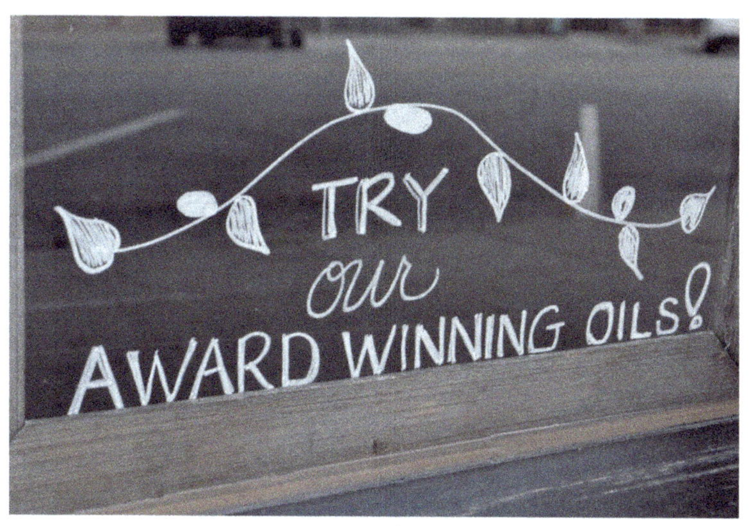

Try my award-winning editing.

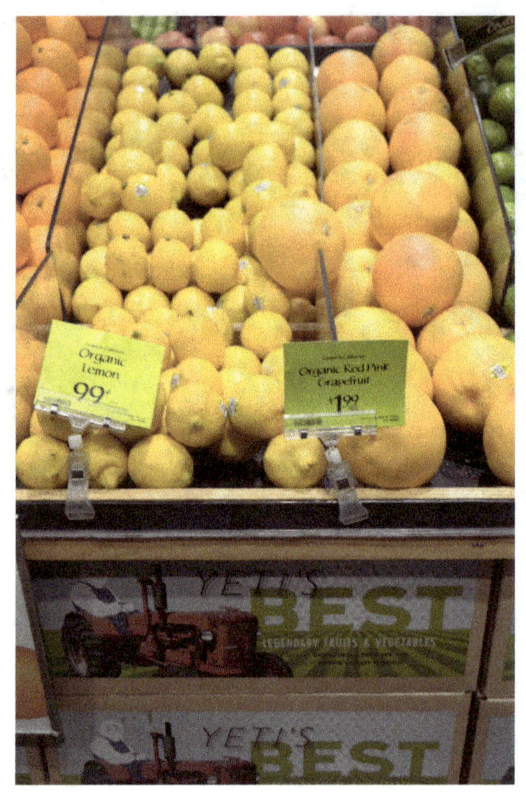

Ascription for Yeti’s longevity.

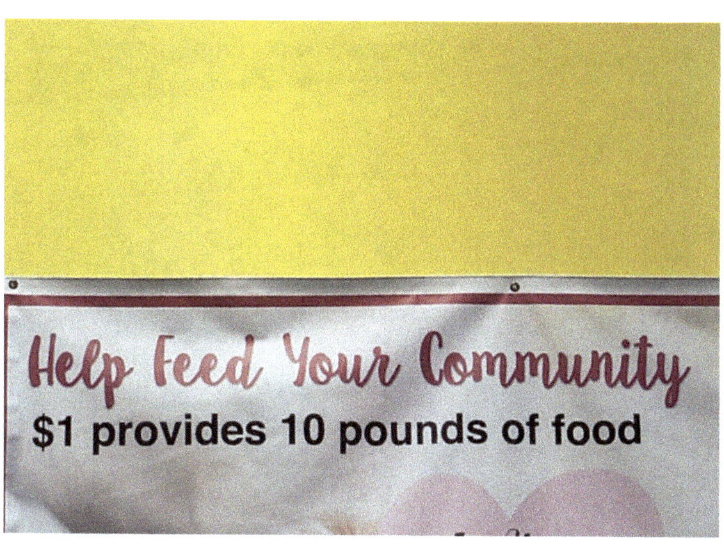

That's not what my receipt reflects.

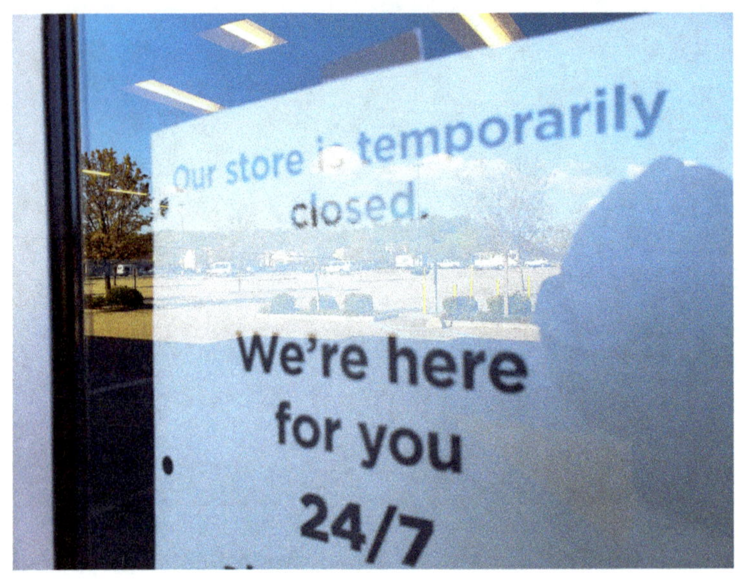

There always never.

SOCIAL DISTANCING
FOR EVERYONE'S SAFETY,
WE ARE ENCOURAGING
SOCIAL DISTANCING.
PLEASE DO YOUR BEST TO
MAINTAIN A MINIMUM
DISTANCE OF 6 FEET FROM
OTHERS WHILE

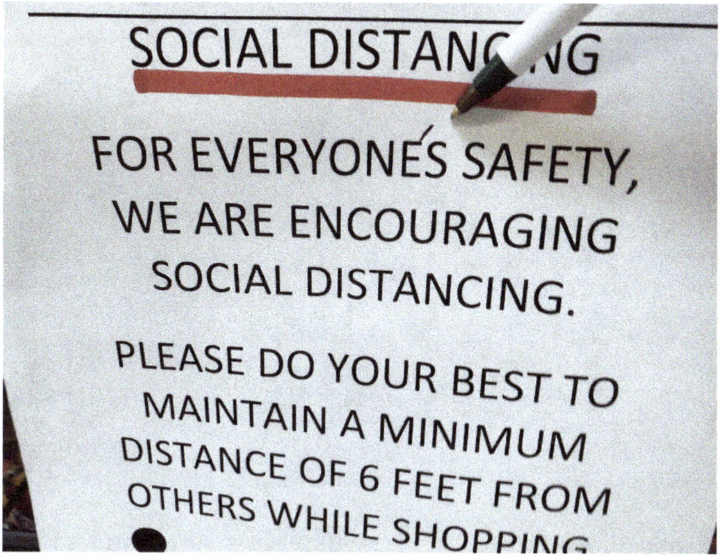

Editor's tag.

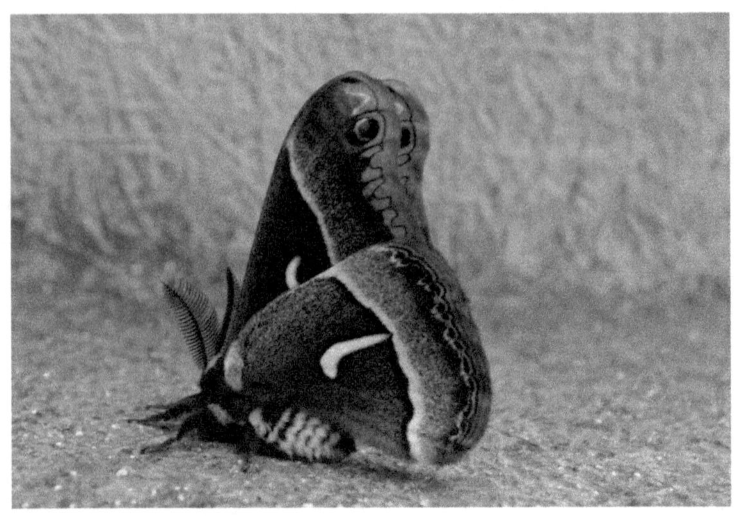

Sweat shops figured out how to place swoosh on a moth.

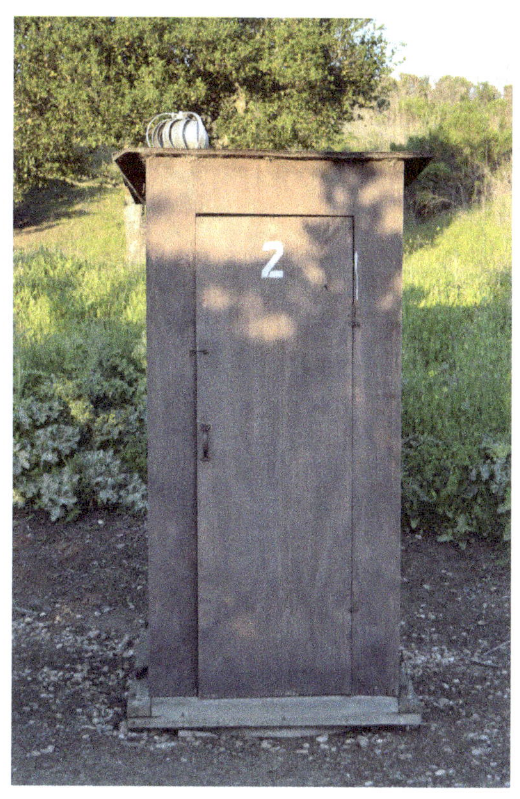

Number 2.

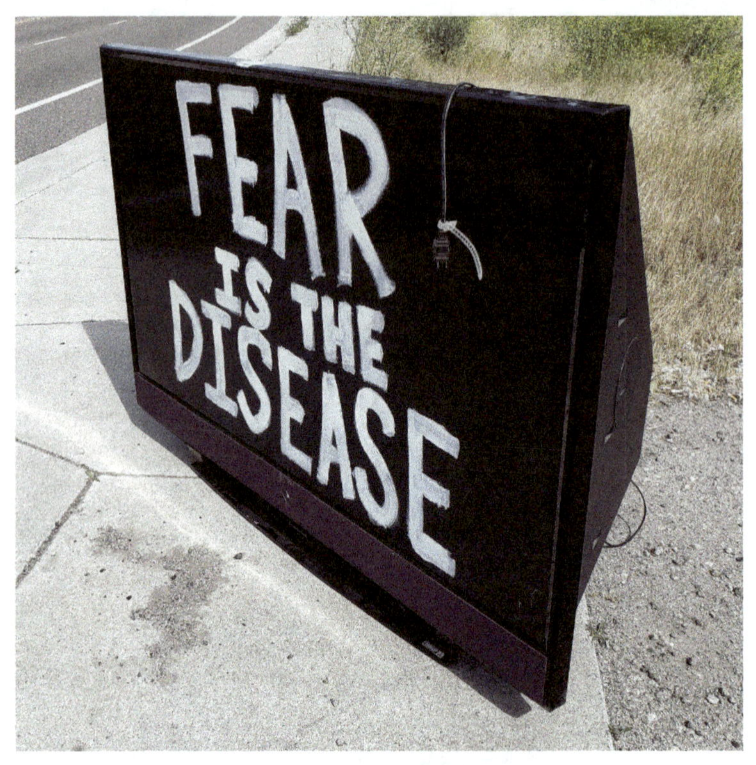

Amen to that.

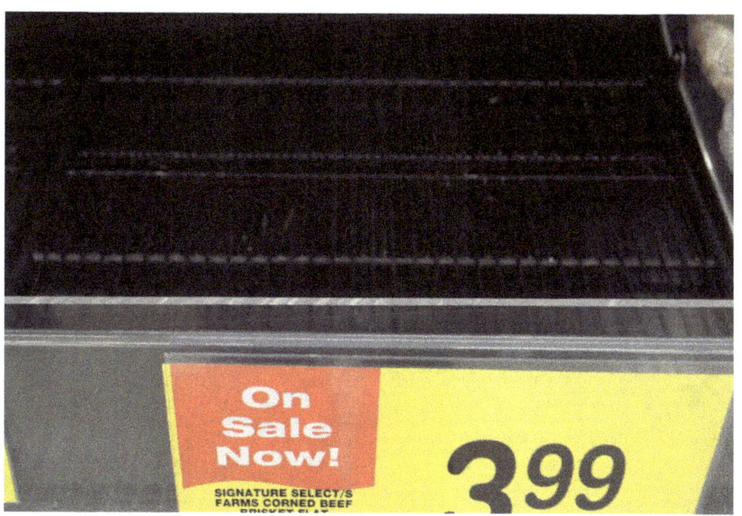

I don’t like it when nothing’s on sale.

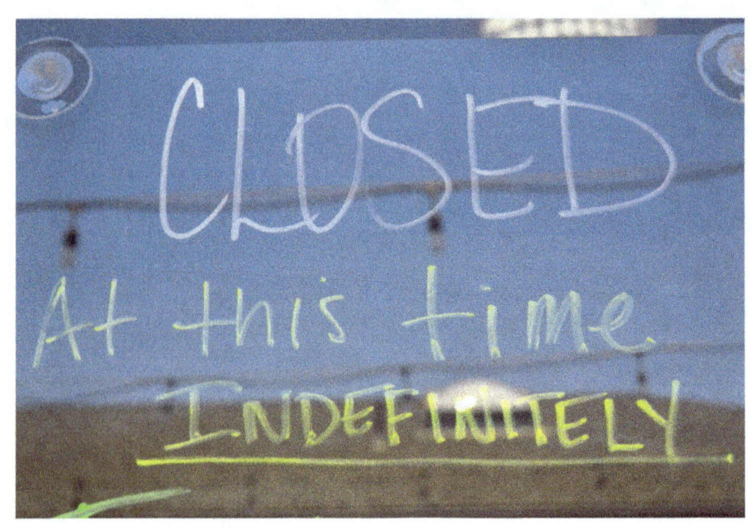

Next time closed definitely.

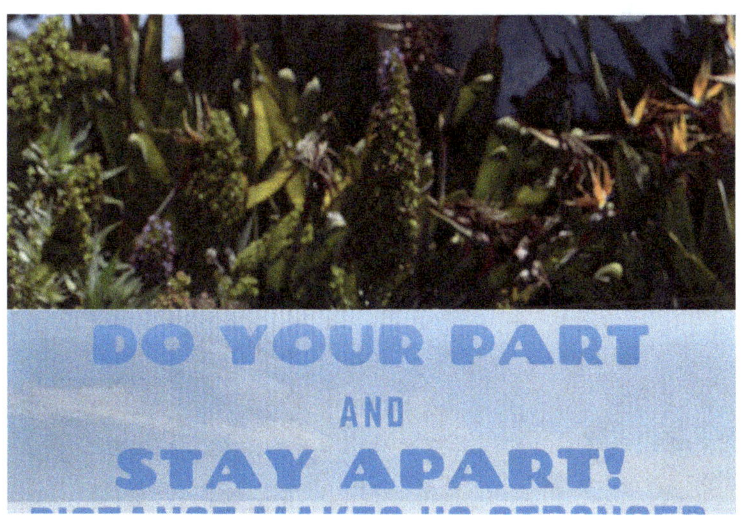

Good advice for couples considering marriage.

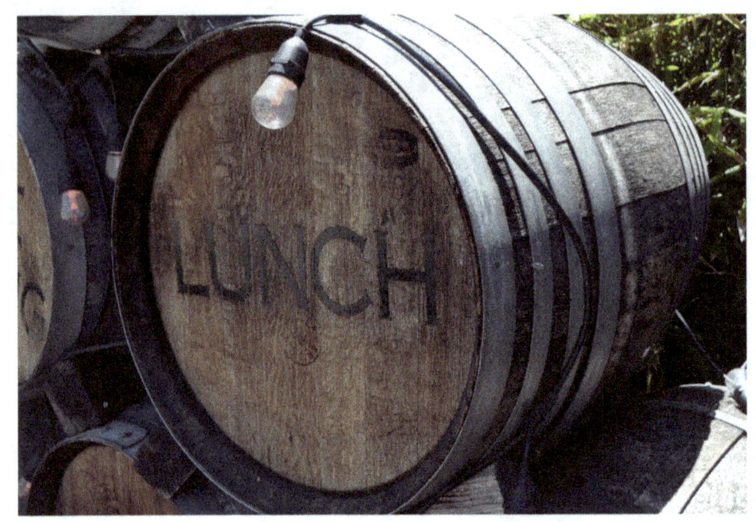

For some, yes.

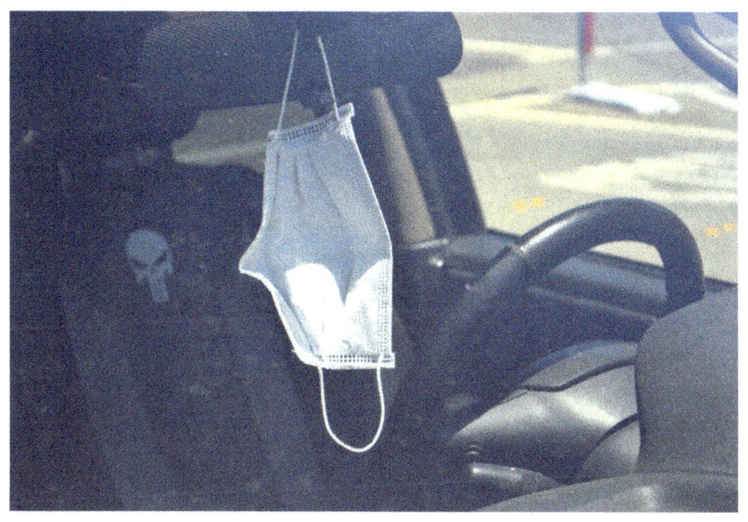

Cause of death.

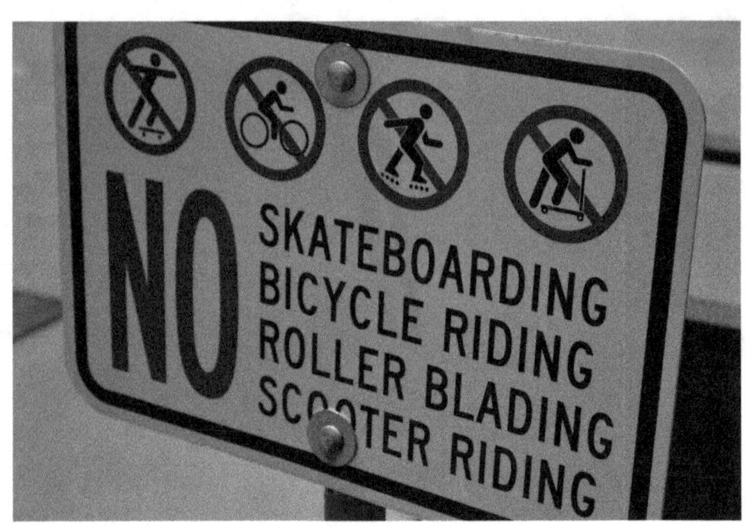

In other words, no having fun.
Good thing I'm a roller skater.
Skating is not a crime.

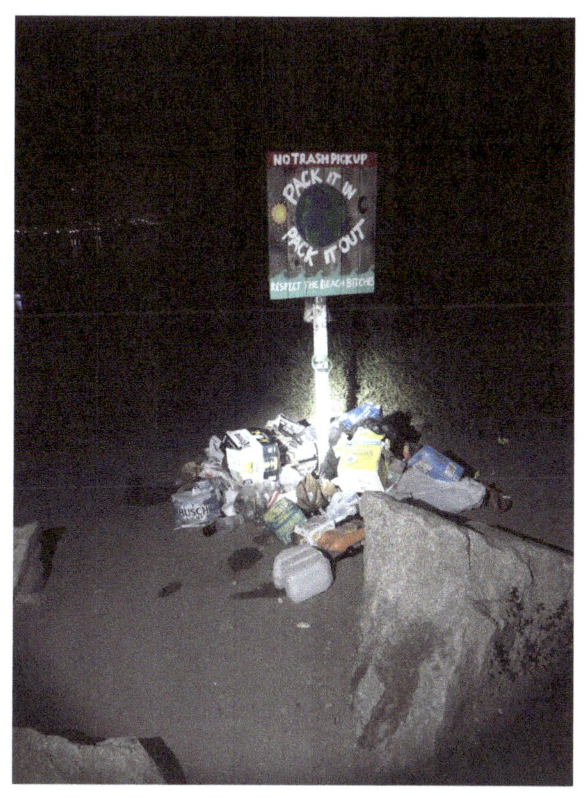

"No leemos Anglais. Scusa."

Photo credit: C. C.

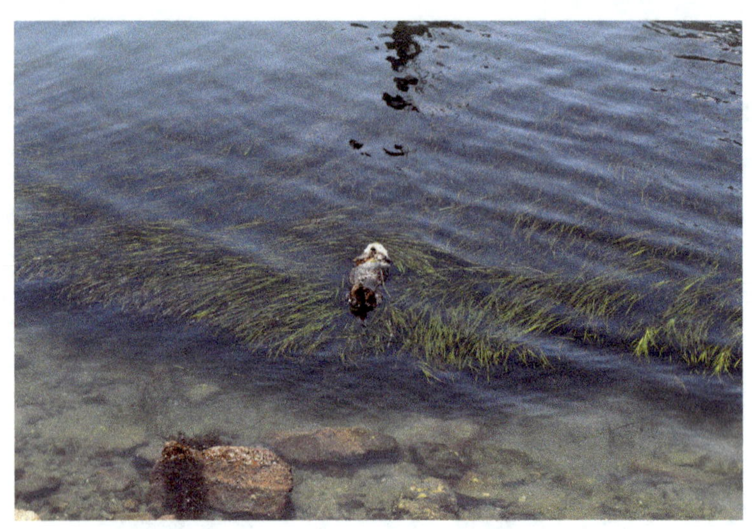

Even sea otters need their beauty sleep.

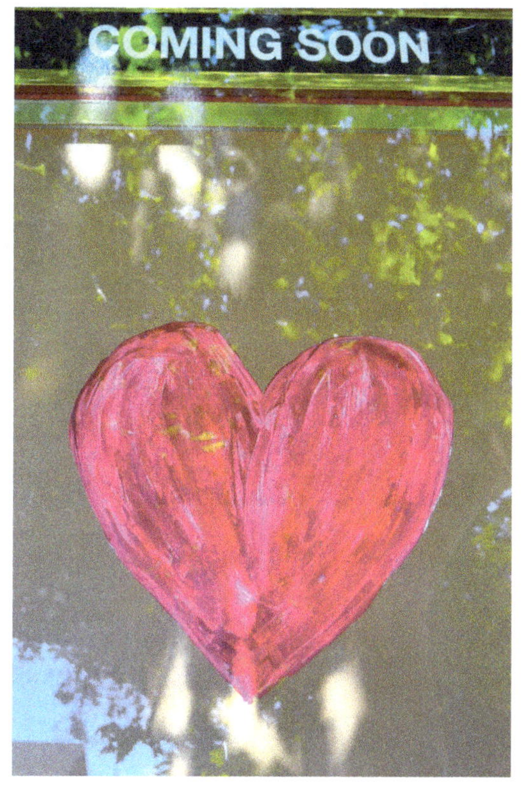

From my heart to yours.

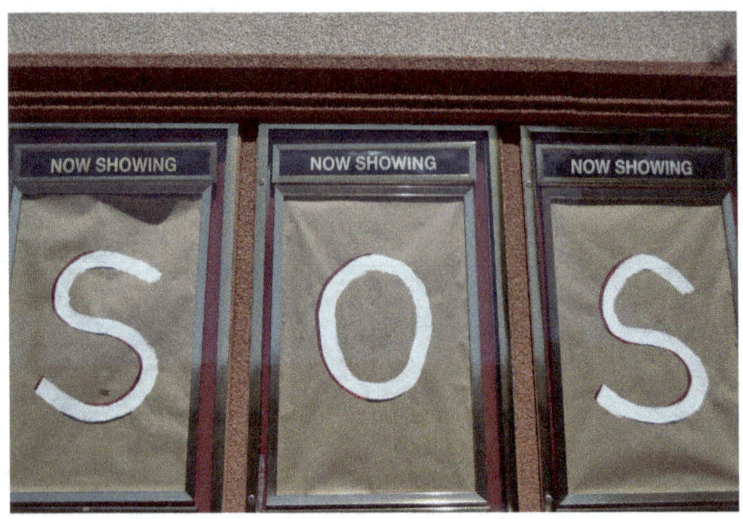

This sign is in front of the US Federal Reserve building every few years.

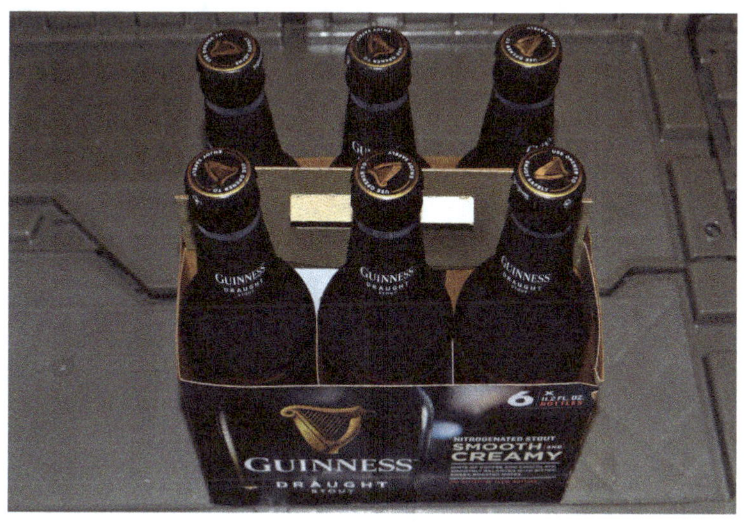

Irishman's Easter basket.

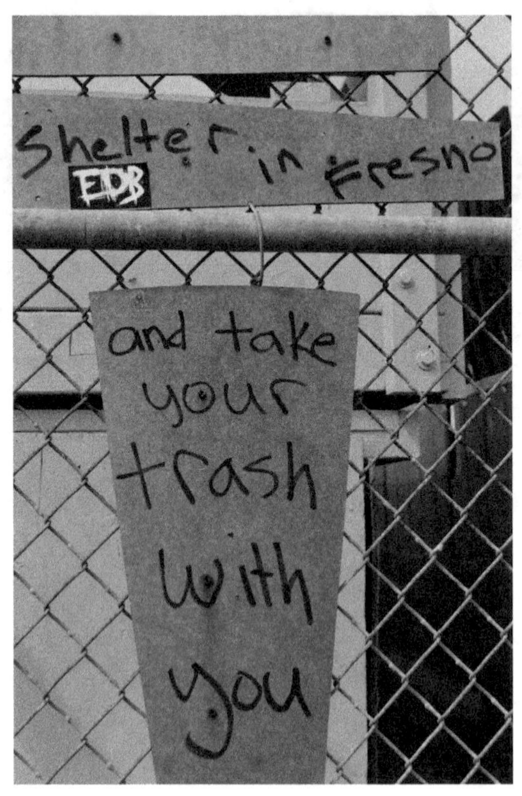

Locals only.

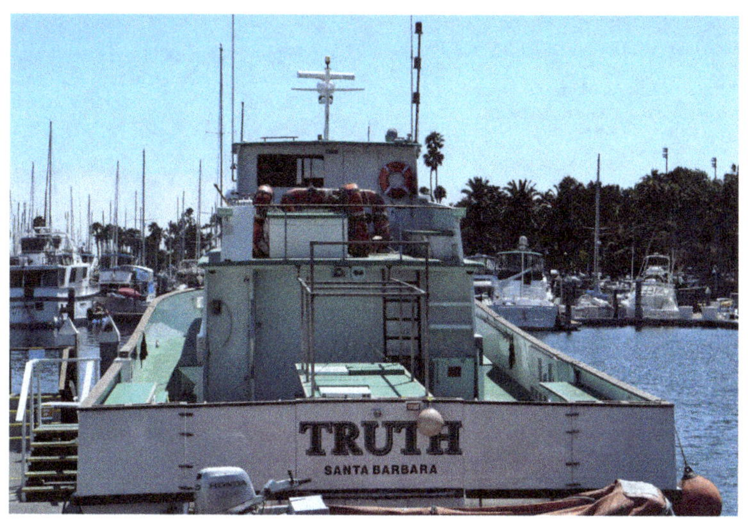

Word.

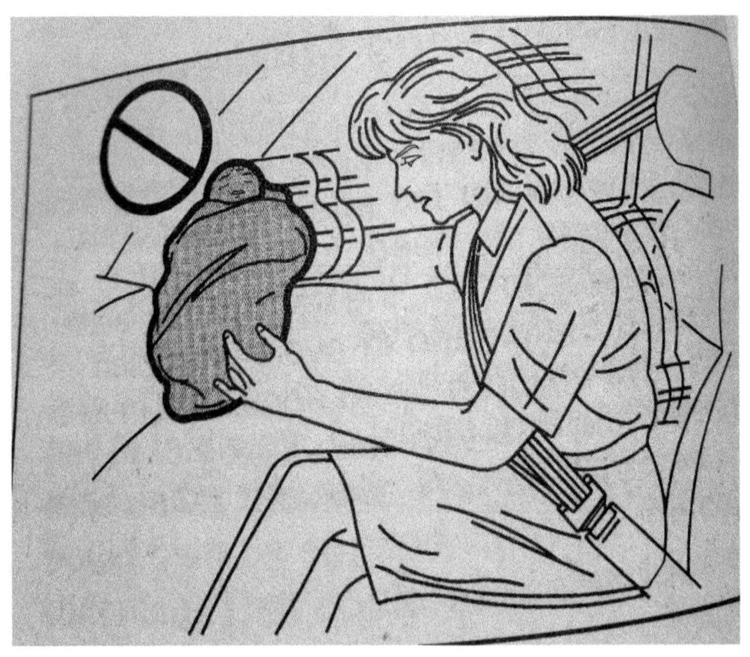

An infant: extra protection for a passenger with no air bag.

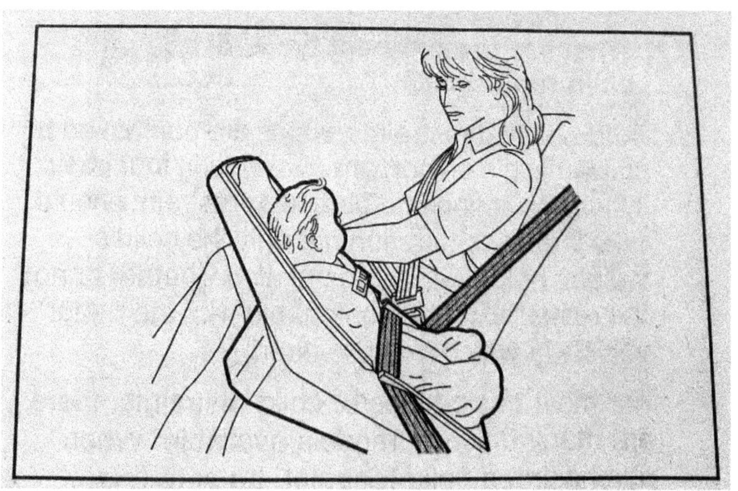

"Mommy's tired. You drive today."

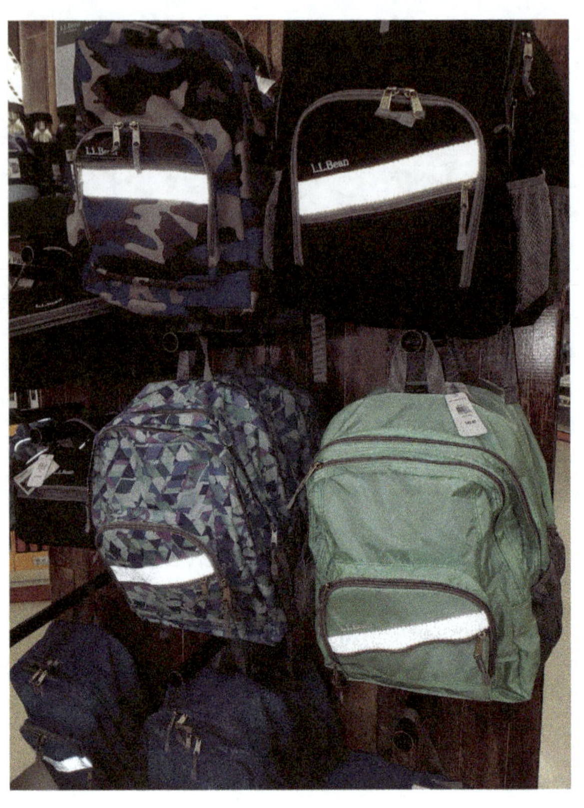

Backpacks for children to carry books from bedroom to living room during a fake pandemic.
Reflect quackery.

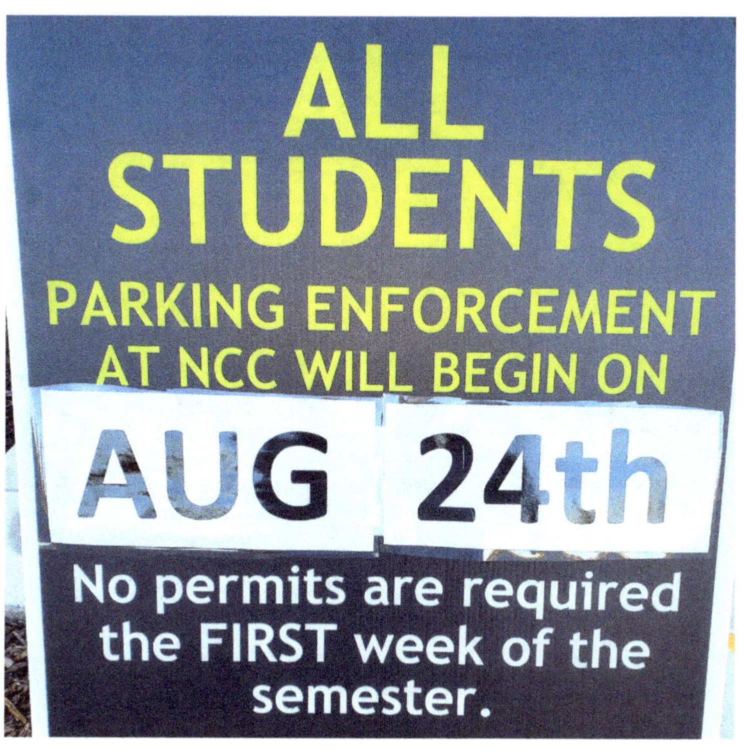

While you're distance learning during a fake pandemic, a permit is required to park in your driveway.

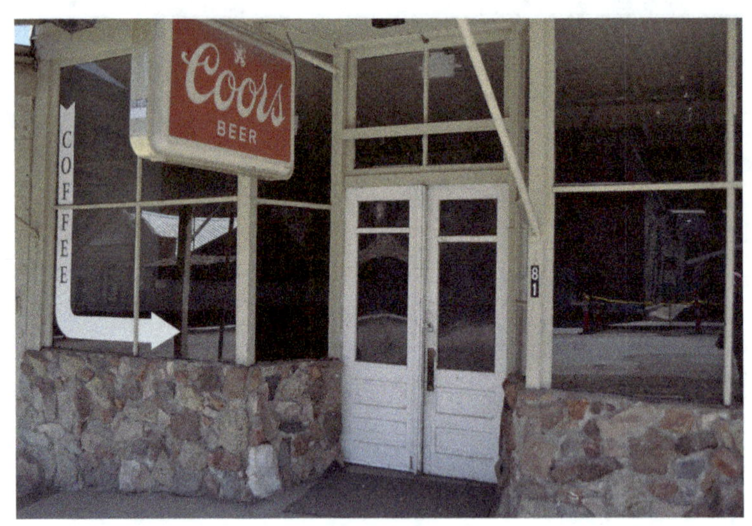

Drug store.

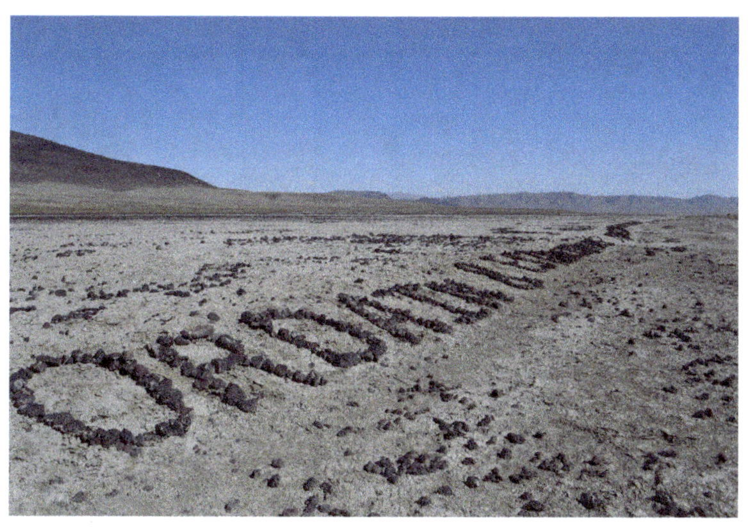

The US Constitution's preamble:
. . . do ordain and establish . . .

Desert graffiti.
Even scorpions know not to cancel culture.

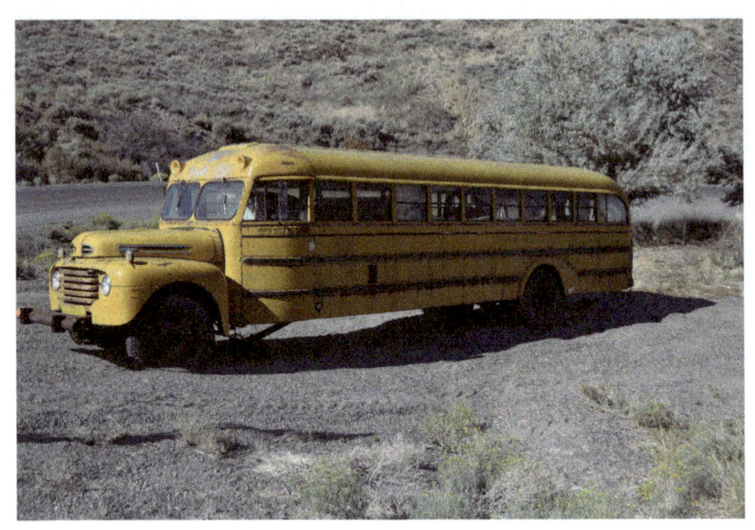

Home schooled bus.

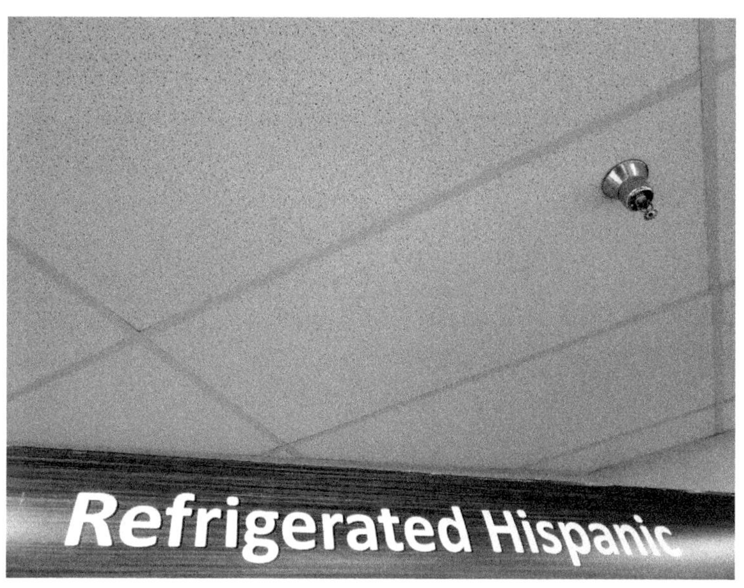

That’s how I like my Hispanics.

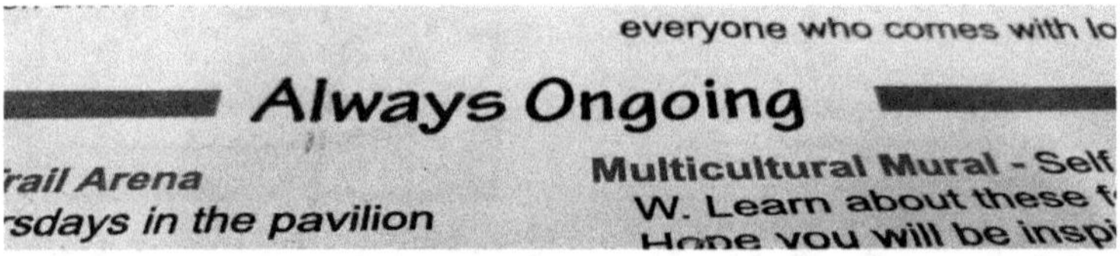

everyone who comes with lo

Always Ongoing

rail Arena
sdays in the pavilion

Multicultural Mural - Self
W. Learn about these f
Hope you will be insp

Always redundant.

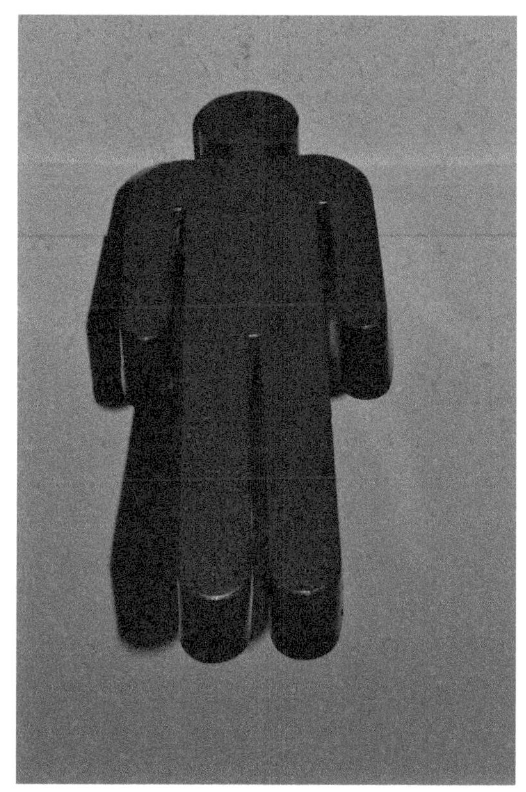

Hang man.

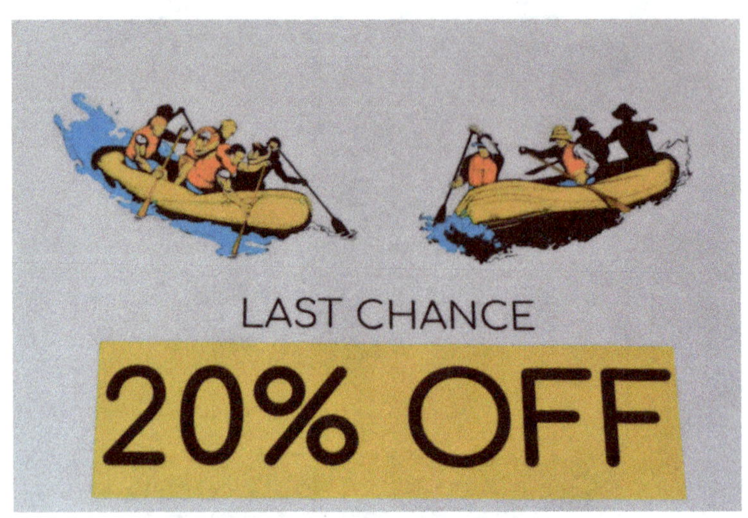

Last chance . . . to stay on the raft.

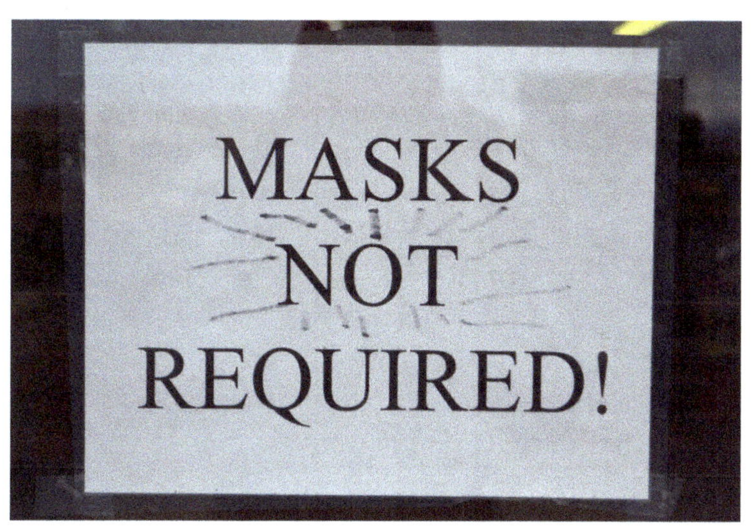

Mormons get it.

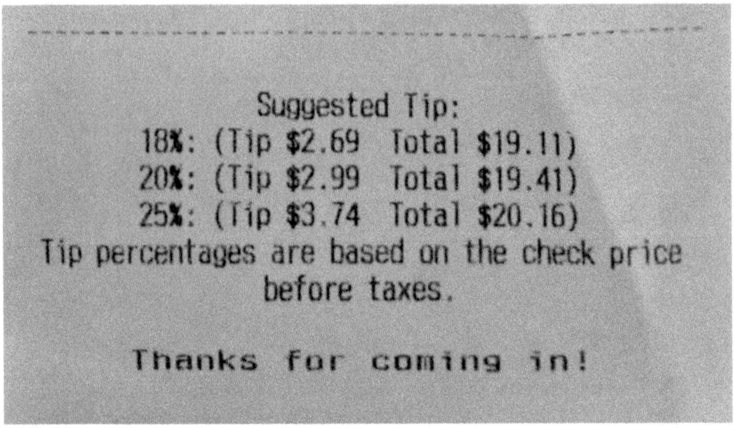

Suggested Tip:
18%: (Tip $2.69 Total $19.11)
20%: (Tip $2.99 Total $19.41)
25%: (Tip $3.74 Total $20.16)
Tip percentages are based on the check price before taxes.

Thanks for coming in!

I suggest 15%.

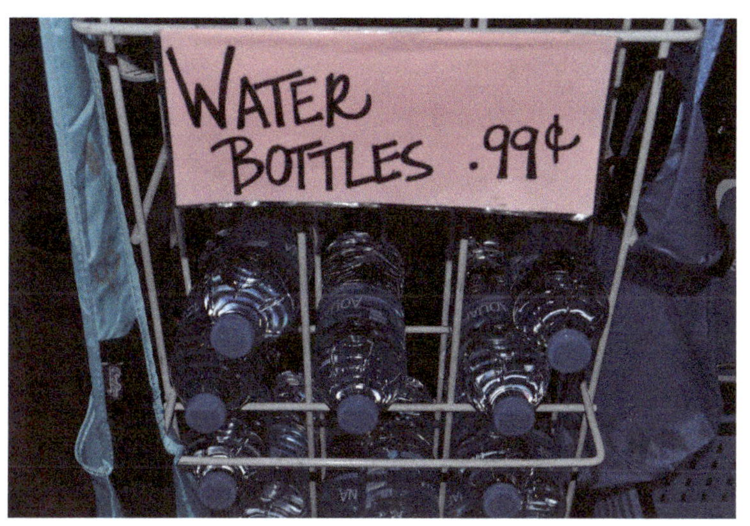

Here’s a penny. Keep the change.

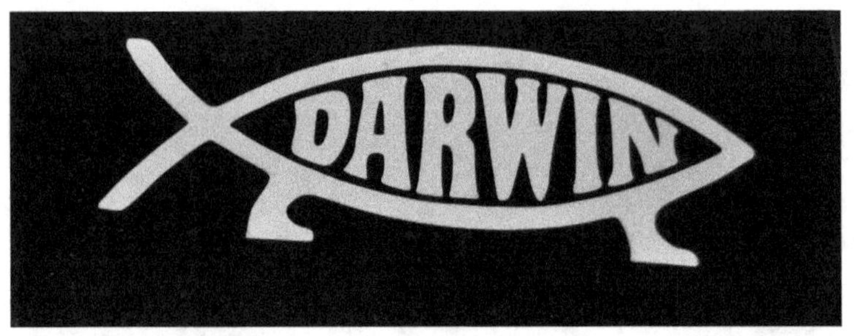

Evolution of brain washing.

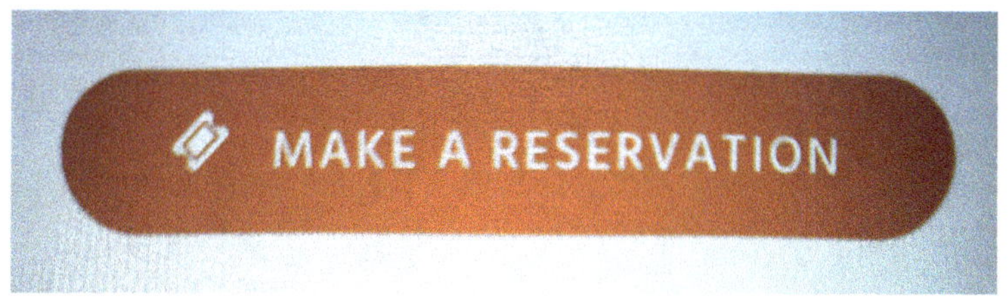

"White Man already did," the Indian said.

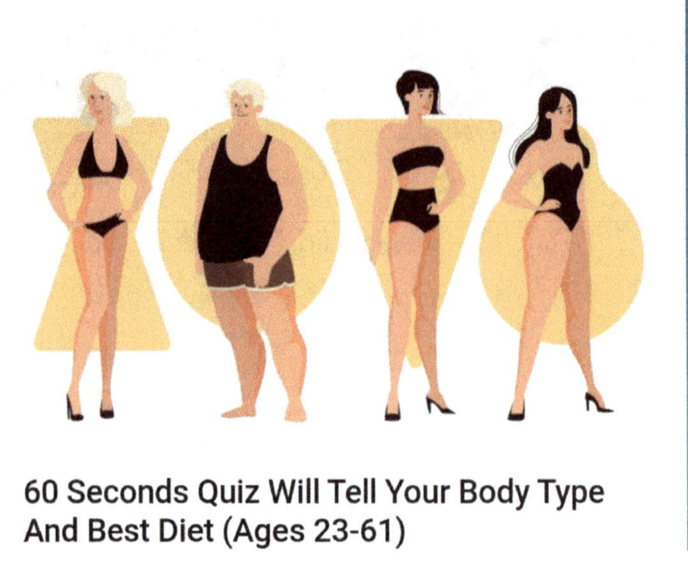

I’m a rectangle.

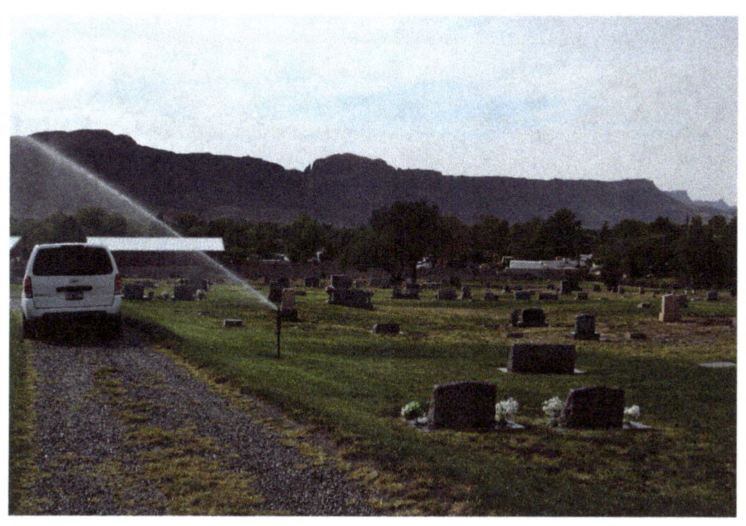

He died a cheap man.

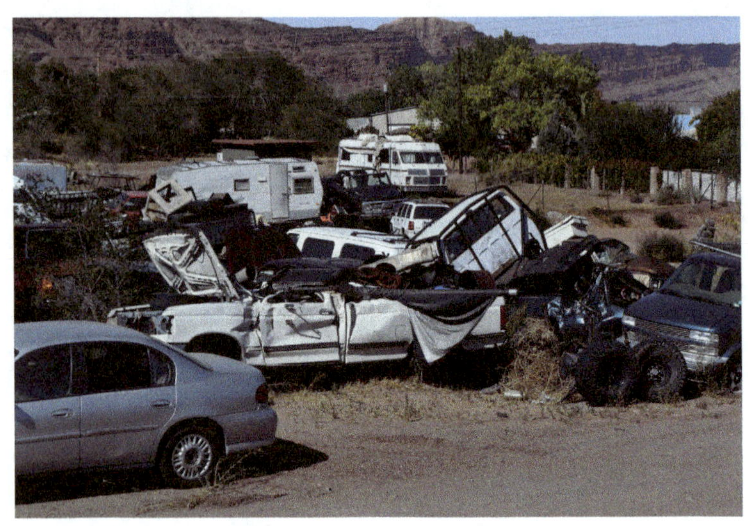

Where your car goes when you can't pay the mechanic's bill.

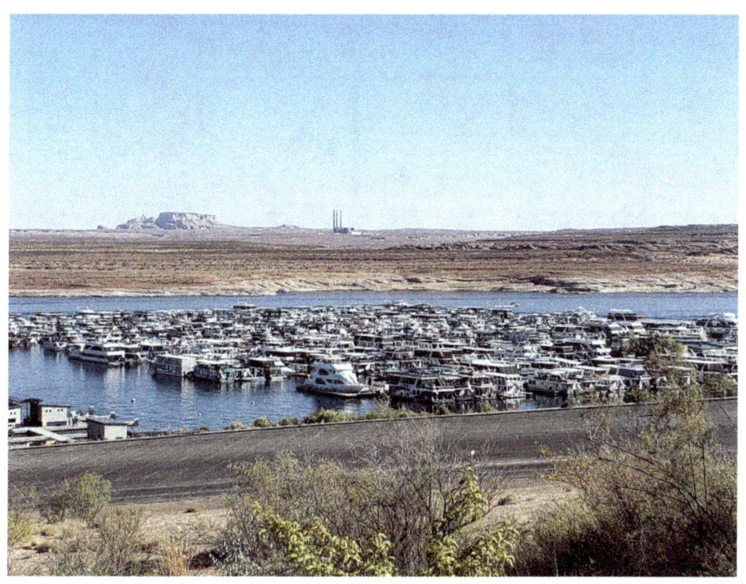

Urban living.

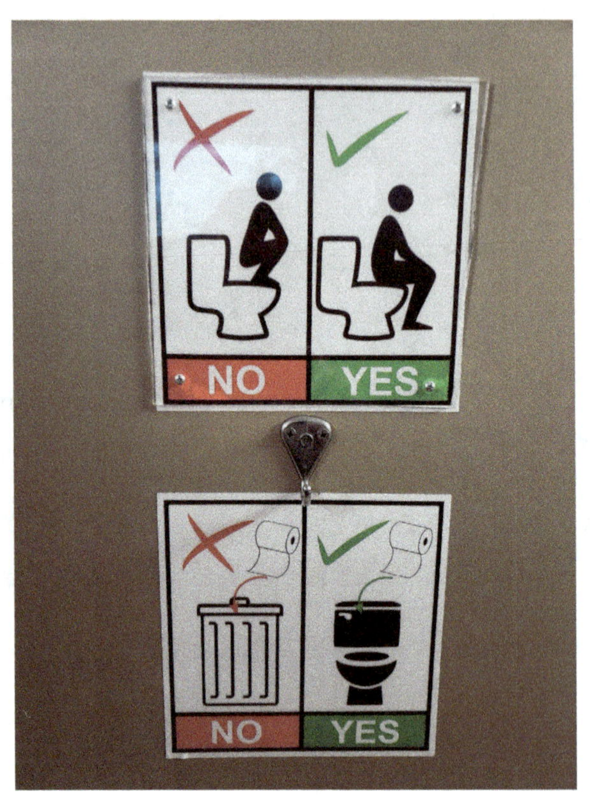

Only in America.

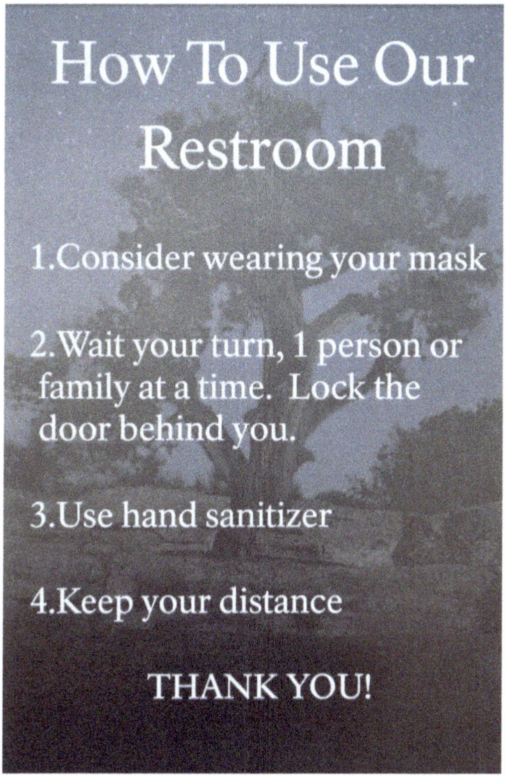

How To Use Our Restroom

1.Consider wearing your mask

2.Wait your turn, 1 person or family at a time. Lock the door behind you.

3.Use hand sanitizer

4.Keep your distance

THANK YOU!

It's a bad sign if you need a sign.

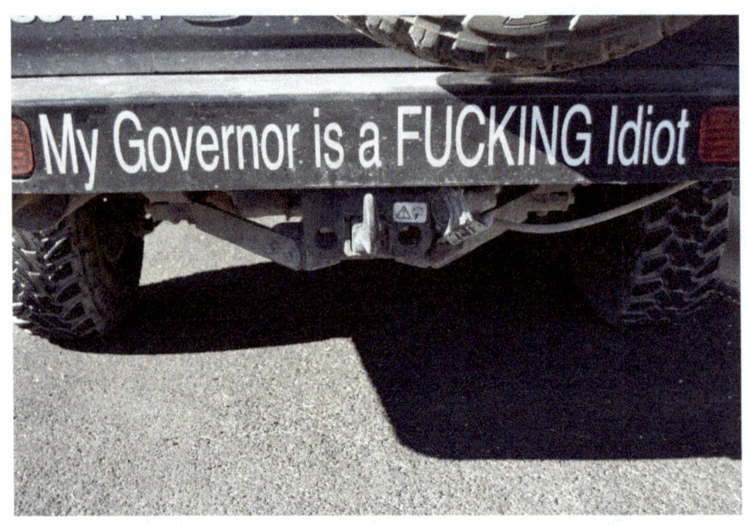

Pick a state.

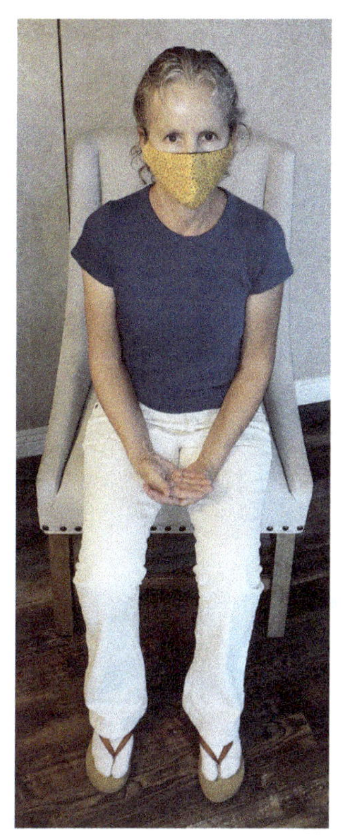

Obedient.

Photo credit: D.

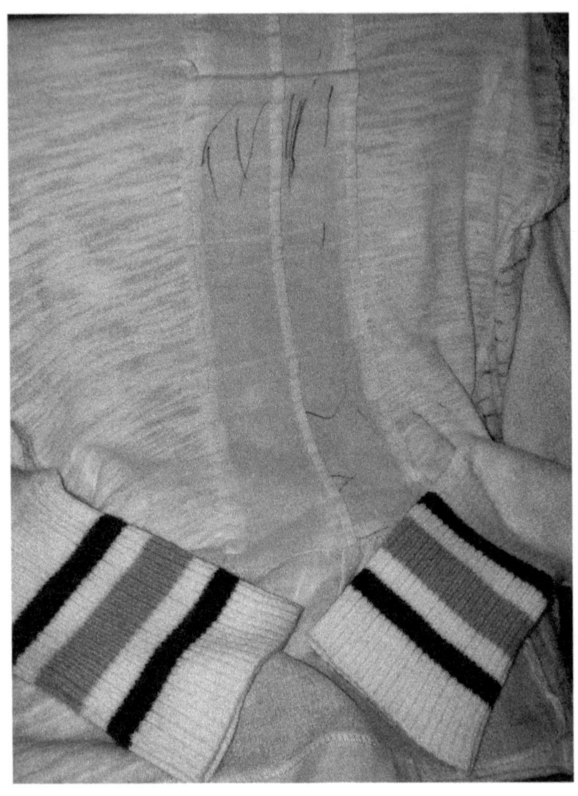

How many blondes does it take to scratch one's back? None. Just a ball-point pen with the cap off. Ugh!! That was my favorite blouse of all time.

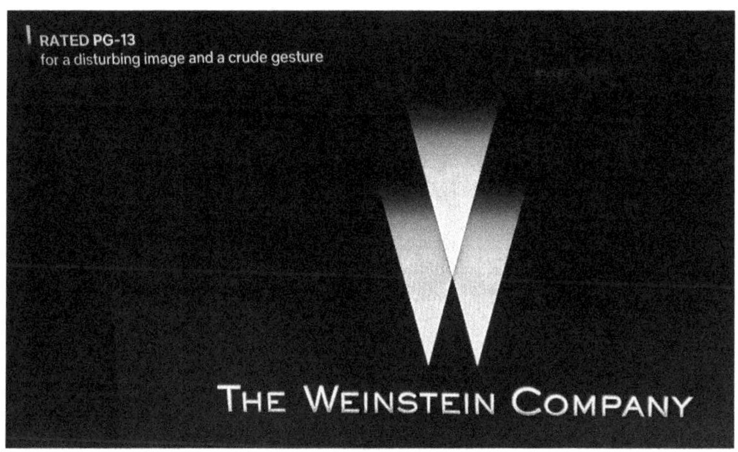

He would know.

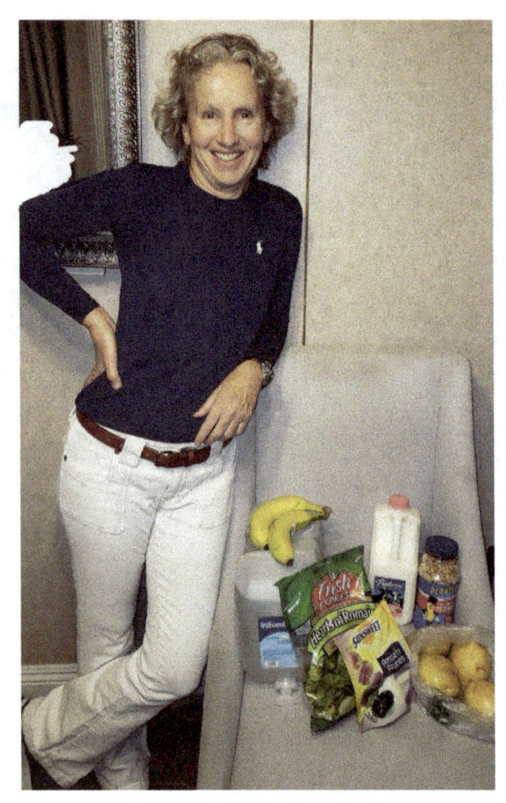

Immunized.

Photo credit: D.

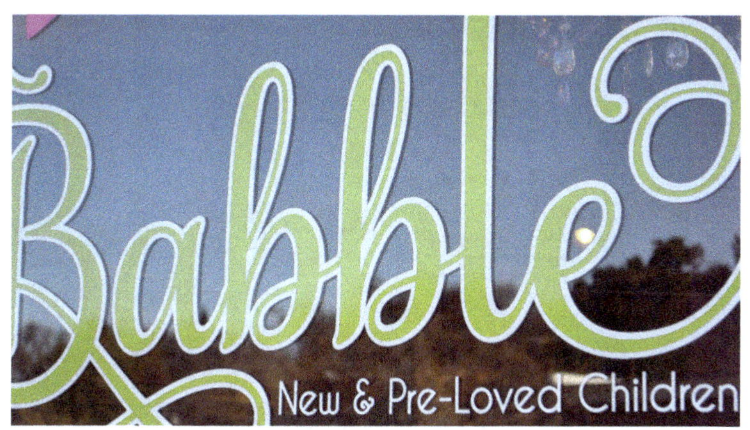

I prefer new children.

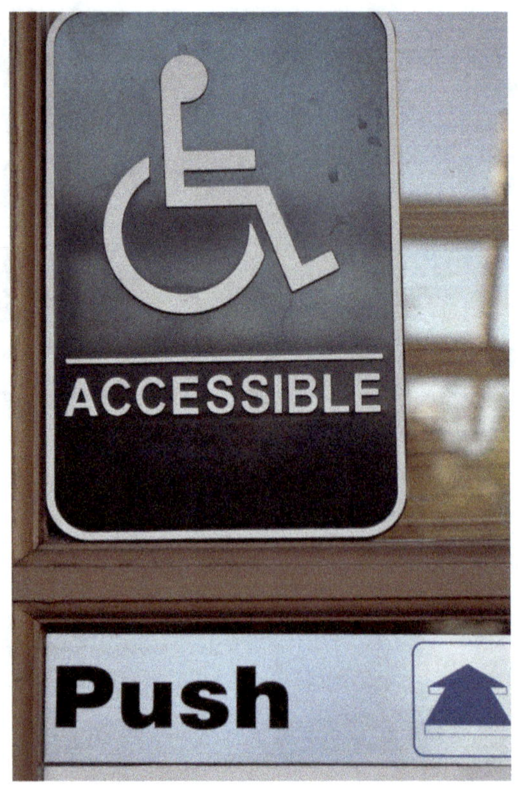

Handicap accessible . . . with a little effort.

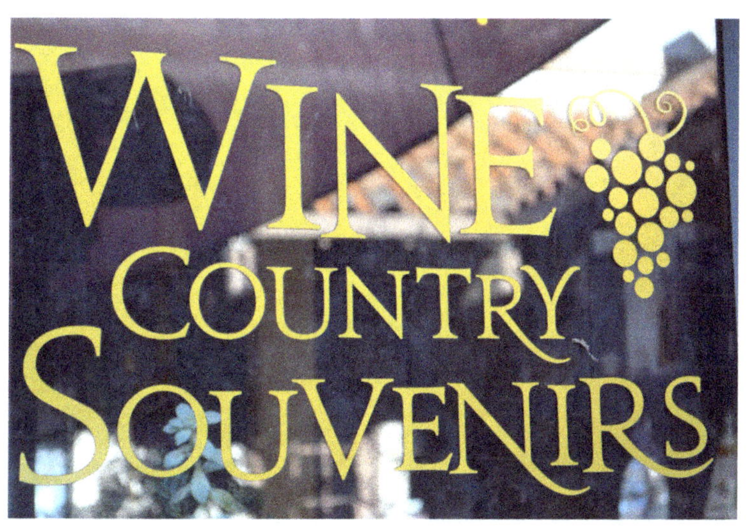

Includes hangovers.

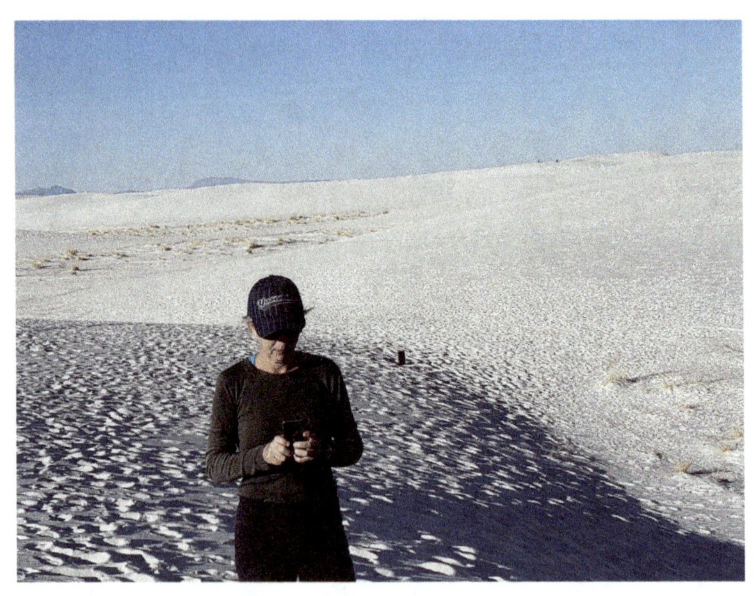

Oblivious.

Photo credit: Alex.

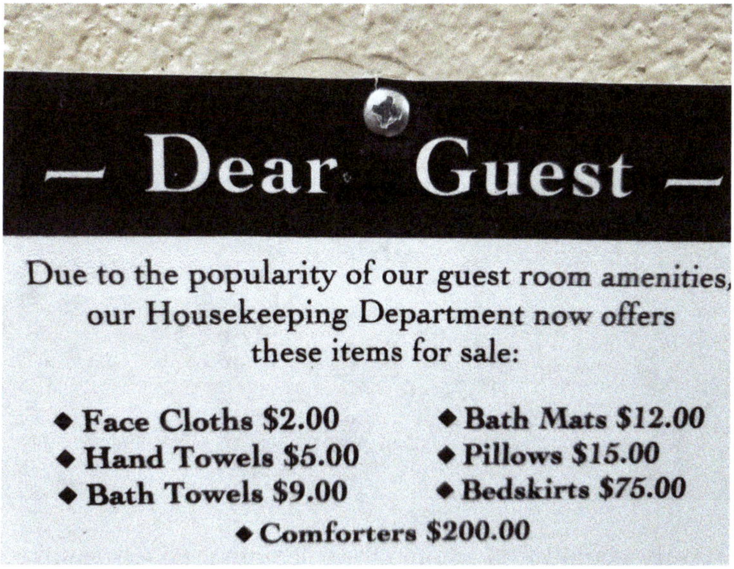

— Dear Guest —

Due to the popularity of our guest room amenities,
our Housekeeping Department now offers
these items for sale:

- **Face Cloths $2.00**
- **Hand Towels $5.00**
- **Bath Towels $9.00**
- **Bath Mats $12.00**
- **Pillows $15.00**
- **Bedskirts $75.00**
- **Comforters $200.00**

In other words, stop stealin' or it'll cost ya'.

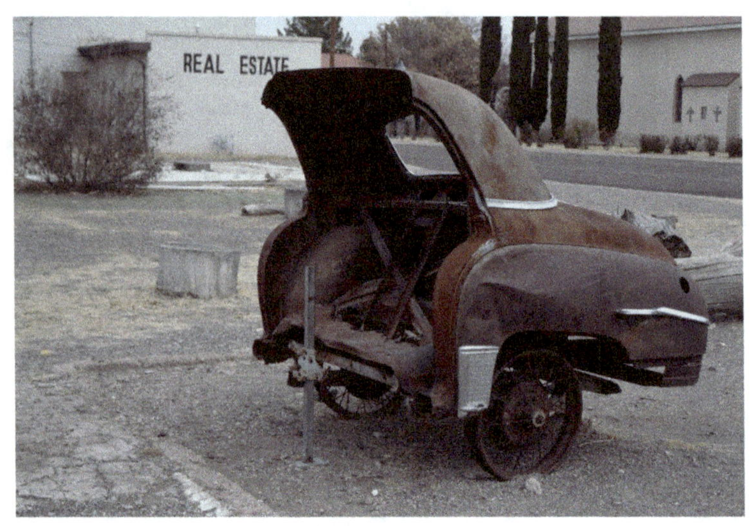

If only I could find a home for sale with a 1/2-car garage.

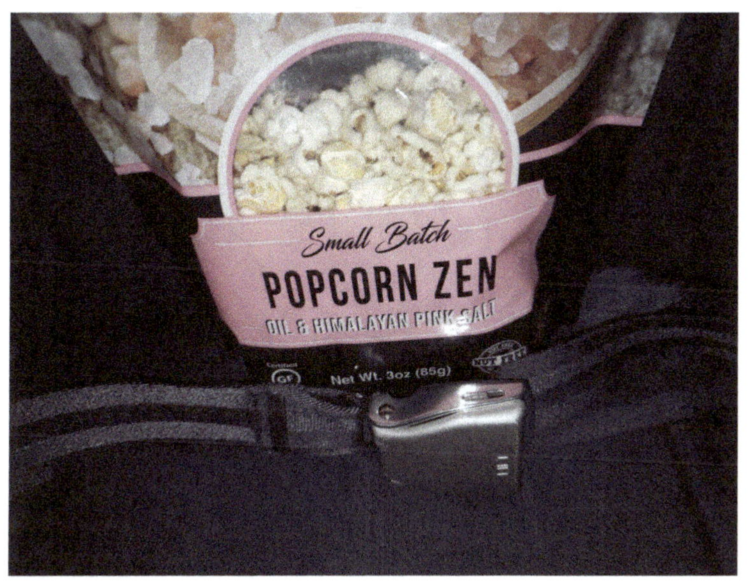

Small Batch
POPCORN ZEN
OIL & HIMALAYAN PINK SALT
Net Wt. 3oz (85g)

Priority.

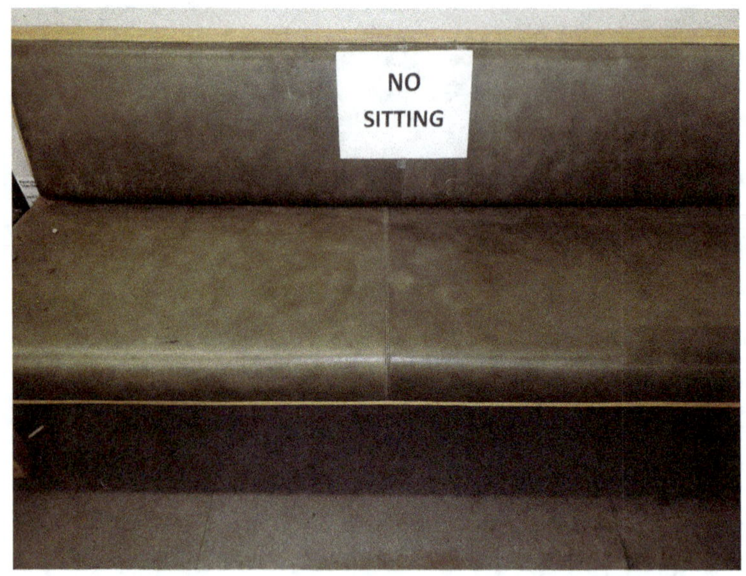

Because that is not what a couch is for.

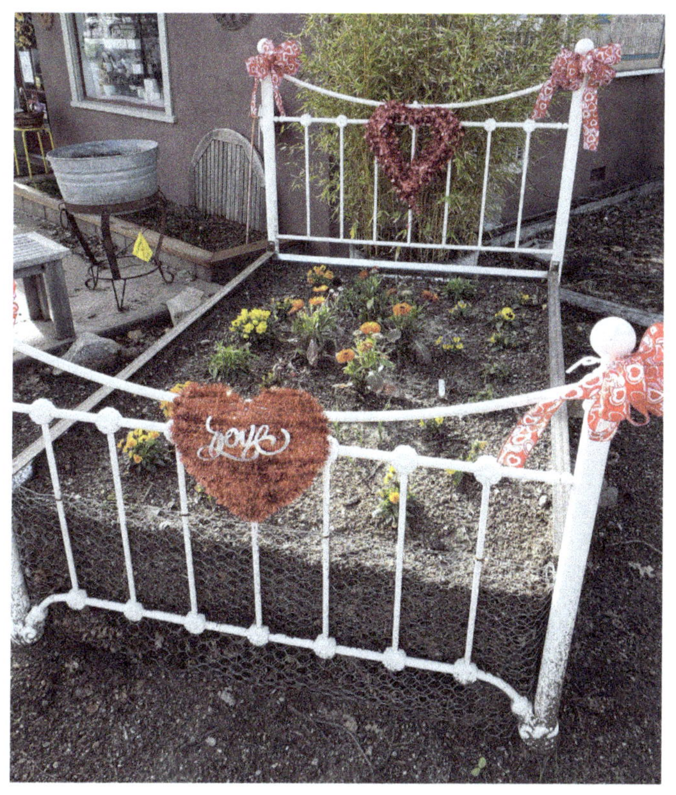

Flower bed.

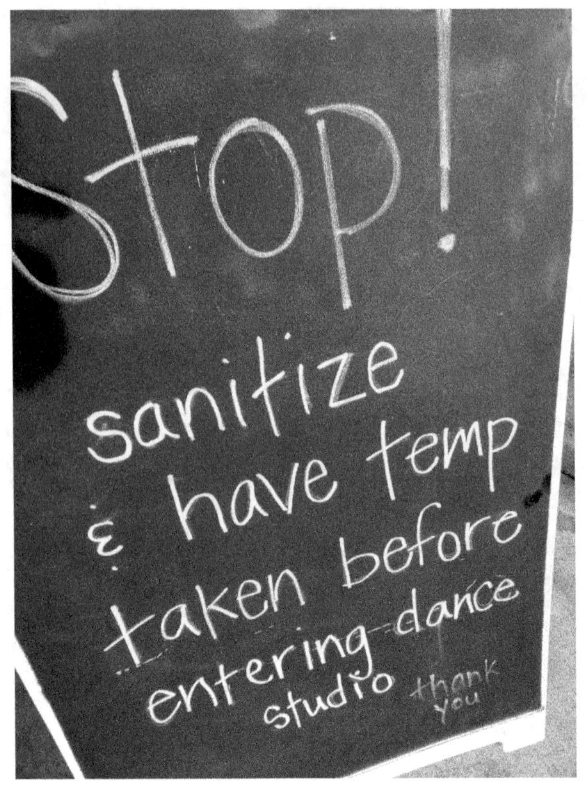

I won't stop, drop, and roll for any quackery.

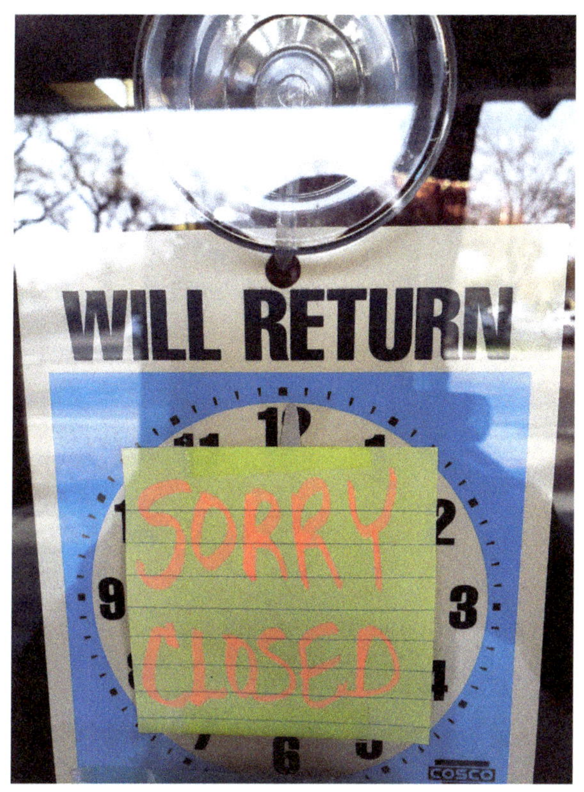

Point of no return.

NATURE'S GUIDE

Your edible landscape consultant

Sounds unappetizing.

ABOUT THE AUTHOR

Arizona photographer and satirist Jeanne "Bean" Murdock brings a new approach to comedy, fusing observational humor with health and fitness knowledge. Performing on roller skates where she can, her improvised physical comedy is one that has never been done before. Jeanne's sassy, naive perspective wins audiences' attention, demanding that "the show must go on."

As much as Jeanne loves to perform, she prefers writing. She is prolific, penning screenplays, books, and of course her own jokes, to name a few.

Originally from Cupertino, California, Jeanne was given the nickname **Bean**, in third grade by her next-door neighbor, simply because it rhymed with Jeanne. She studied physical education at California Polytechnic State University in San Luis Obispo, and then started **BEAN**FIT Health and Fitness Services in 1992. Three years later, Jeanne was diagnosed with celiac disease, a condition that she included in her teachings. For 22 years she was a health and fitness professional who also happened to be a comedian. Now, she is a comedian who happens to be a health and fitness expert.

Qualifications:
California Polytechnic State University, San Luis Obispo
Bachelor of Science in Physical Education: concentration in Commercial/Corporate Fitness
Graduation Date: June 1991

San Diego State University, San Diego, CA
Nutrition Didactic Program
Verified: May 2002

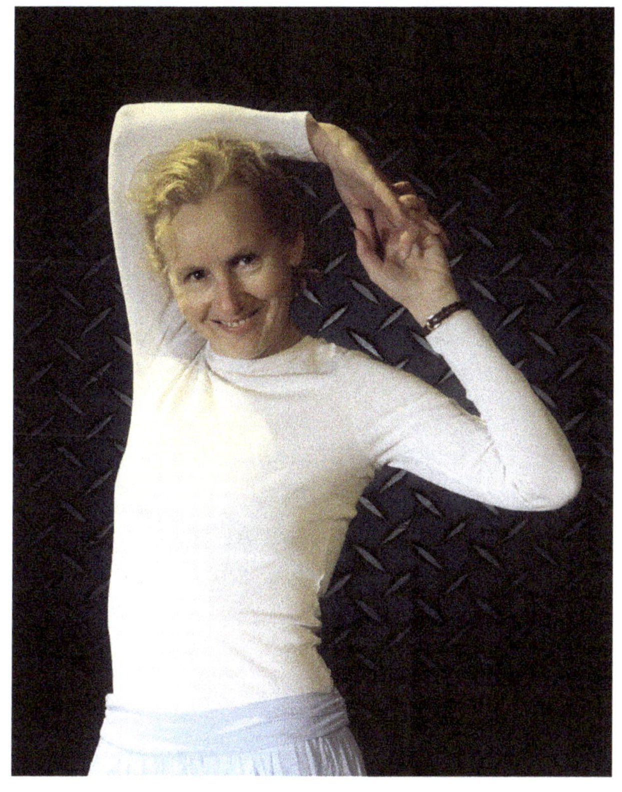

Image by Jim Tyler, edited by Greg Heller

Questions? Comments? Please feel free to write or call Jeanne "Bean" Murdock anytime at:

PO Box 372
Cornville, AZ 86325
Phone: 408-203-7643
Website: www.JeanneMurdock.com
E-mail: laugh@JeanneMurdock.com

Other books by Jeanne "Bean" Murdock
(via BEANFIT Publishing):

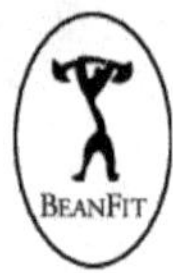

The Every Excuse in the Book Book: How to Benefit from Exercising, by Overcoming Your Excuses
Successful Dating at Last! A Workbook for Understanding Each Other
It's Hard to Find Good Help These Days: A Customer Service Manual for Businesses
That's a Bunch of Quackery! How to Avoid Being Pick-pocketed by Misleading Claims in the Fitness Industry
Serial Good Samaritan
Memorable Greetings

Co-author of Carole Breton's autobiography
My Guardian Angel Wears Antiperspirant
(Stinky Ghost Cat Books 2018)

Not-so ghost writer of Ted Gilbert's autobiography
Barefoot NOMAD
(POGA Publishing 2019)

Not-so ghost writer of Babe Daley's autobiography
Arizona Native
(Isley Publishing 2023)

www.ingramcontent.com/pod-product-compliance
Lightning Source LLC
LaVergne TN
LVHW050539100826
845148LV00002B/619
9798986094823